T0304914

Exploding Tomatoes
and Other Stories

Exploding Tomatoes and Other Stories

The Food and Flavours of Southern Italy

SOPHIE GRIGSON

First published in 2024 by Headline Home
an imprint of Headline Publishing Group

1

Cataloguing in Publication Data is available from the British Library.

Hardback ISBN 978 1 4722 9629 0
eISBN 978 1 4722 9631 3

Illustrations © Kavel Rafferty 2024

Copy editor: Annie Lee
Proofreader: Anne Sheasby
Indexer: Ruth Ellis
Designed and set by EM&EN

Printed and bound in Great Britain by Clays Ltd, Elcograf S.p.A.

HEADLINE PUBLISHING GROUP
An Hachette UK Company
Carmelite House
50 Victoria Embankment
London EC4Y 0DZ

www.headline.co.uk
www.hachette.co.uk

For Florrie and Sid, always.

Contents

Introduction

It's been more than four years now since chance, luck, fate, call it what you will, landed me in the small town of Ceglie Messapica in the heart of Puglia. Then I knew nobody; now I walk through the streets nodding to this and that acquaintance, stopping to chat for a moment with those I know better. I know the shortest backstreet routes to the Saturday market, the pet shop, and Ceglie's finest *pizzeria*. I've just about mastered the difference between *pesca* (peach) and *pesce* (fish), between *uva* (grape) and *uova* (egg). Local shopkeepers slip a little something extra into my bag, an aubergine perhaps at Michele's *fruttivendolo*, the last two conger steaks at Antonio's *pescheria* to make a little *sughetto* for my pasta.

In short, this feels like home. It is home, a happy one. I will always be the outsider here but that allows me odd indulgences. My lack of housewifely prowess, for instance, is forgiven by my neighbour who frequently sweeps my front step after she gives hers its essential daily clean. The shared experience of successive Covid lockdowns has smoothed off the sharp corners of my foreignness.

For much of this time those lockdowns and Italian bureaucracy have kept me close to home, but now I am free to venture further afield. My faithful purple aubergine of a car has been returned to service with its brand-new Italian numberplates. Cooler weather has set in, tourists have mostly vanished. Food, as ever, is my medium for discovery, containing as it does the DNA of towns, villages and families, carrying traces of history, of terrain, of culture and climate.

I had intended to make one grand sweep of a journey to explore the most southerly parts of southern Italy, from Santa Maria di Leuca at the bottom of the heel, travelling slowly up and over the boot's instep to Reggio Calabria, positioned right at the toe. A magnificent adventure through the parts of Italy that comparatively few foreign tourists ever reach. My grand tour, if you will, hugging the coastline then darting inland to hills and mountains and hidden villages and towns. Then one late autumn afternoon I realised that my hand had shot up into the air as the café proprietor asked if anyone could give a home to a kitten in need. Felix purred into my life, followed six weeks later by Juno. Well, it's only fair to give a little cat a friend to play with. Suddenly the big plan fractured down into small five- or six-day excursions, taken throughout the cooler months from October to April over two years.

These excursions have taken me to a host of little fishing ports, past long windswept beaches, ancient pine forests, into the wild hills of Basilicata and its main town of Matera where the former cave slums now house chic boutique hotels, up into Calabria's high Sila, famed for its chestnuts and mushrooms, down to the golden sands of its coast, and on to the bergamot orchards clustering around Reggio.

I've been tipped off to a particularly fine lamb pie in Matera and to the crisp-fried *cruschi* peppers of Basilicata. I've wound up squiggling hair-pinned mountain roads to revisit Camigliatello Silano, home to one of the best *porcini* festivals in the Mezzogiorno. I've tracked down the origins of the stunning smoked ricotta that I've dreamt about since a first beguiling mouthful two years before (Crotone, just in case you want to get some yourself). I had a yen to retrace a little of my first perambulations in Calabria some forty years ago, this time in more comfort and minus the backpack. Lack of time thwarted my attempt to follow my younger self (and boyfriend of the moment) on a long, bumpy bus ride up to the

Certosa di Serra San Bruno, a monastery perfectly perched on the edge of the Aspromonte hills, where we discovered to my dismay that the enthusiastic guidebook had failed to mention that women weren't allowed across the monks' strictly masculine threshold. I returned to the small town of Stilo, where I was almost arrested. With hindsight, I see that my crime was no worse than being a young bleach-blonde foreigner waiting for a bus in a town where nothing ever happened and the *carabinieri* were bored witless. On my own doorstep I stumbled on an exquisitely simple dish of exploding tomatoes. I'm sorry to say that Santa Maria de Leuca, where the Adriatic meets the Ionian, is still on my hit list.

The E90 highway swishes from Taranto in Puglia all the way around the Gulf of Taranto right down to Reggio Calabria, hugging the shoreline for much of its 500 kilometres. Almost as soon as you cross the border between Puglia and Basilicata the colour of the earth changes from rust red brown to yellow-grey clay. To the north-west rise the *calanchi*, the bare, ghostly foothills of Basilicata's mountainous interior. The food begins to change too. Not dramatically, but little hints of the sweet and sour legacy from the Moorish occupation of Sicily creep in, and most notably, the rise and rise of the sausage. By the time you dine in Calabria, sausages in one form or another are enshrined in full glory in practically every meal. Only the hordes of fish restaurants fringing the turquoise waters of the Ionian ignore the sausage, revelling instead in the pearly fresh harvest of the sea.

Along the way, I've been helped, fed and entertained by so many kind, generous, fascinating people both in real life, on the page and on the internet. Books and TV programmes about the food and cooking of Sicily are ten a penny. Puglia's cuisine is beginning to be discovered abroad, but the equally delicious foods of Basilicata and Calabria remain relatively unknown. The cooks, farmers and fishermen of Italy's south have created a panoply of good eating, emerging from centuries of harsh poverty. It may not be as sophisticated as northern Italian food, but it is honest and joyous and ripe for recognition.

Sophie Grigson
July 2023

Ingredients

A brief guide to some southern Italian ingredients used in the recipes and possible substitutes for those that are hard to find elsewhere.

Anchovies

Alici or *acciughe*, fresh or preserved, salted, in oil or marinated; for such teeny, inoffensive silvery fish they sure are complicated. They also make a massive difference to much simple food. So here is my whistle-stop guide to choosing your anchovies:

The words *alici* and *acciughe* are used pretty much interchangeably in Italy, though apparently there is a technical piscine difference. It doesn't need to worry the cook.

Preserved salted anchovies: When a recipe lists plain 'anchovy', you can safely assume that a preserved, salted anchovy is required. My anchovy of choice, and the most commonly available, is the sort that comes in oil in a small tin or jar. Olive oil is better than sunflower oil, but both are acceptable. Anchovies may also be stored in salt alone, often whole. Filleting them is easy, but why bother when the tinned ones are just as good and ready to go?

Fresh anchovies on the other hand are just that – the whole, fresh-from-the-sea, unpreserved silvery anchovy. They do benefit, in most recipes, from cleaning and filleting. Not difficult, though a bit icky. Also oddly satisfying. See page 27.

They **must** be used either on the day they are bought or at most the day after.

Marinated anchovies are fresh silvery anchovy fillets that have been preserved either in dilute vinegar or lemon juice. The ones you buy ready marinated from the fishmonger or deli or supermarket can be over-acidic. I'm never going to buy them again, because home-marinated anchovies are so totally superior – if you find fresh anchovies for sale, turn straight to page 26 and make your own.

Capers

Capers grow wild and free throughout the south of Italy, lurking in stony ground that produces little else. For centuries they have provided cheap piquancy for those that make the time to pick them. For those of us who have to buy them, the best option are the smallest capers (nonpareilles), preserved in brine or vinegar. I ignore jars of salt-heavy capers. They need too much work rinsing and soaking them into palatable submission. Despite what many food writers insist, they are not superior in flavour.

Cheeses

Italy produces a clutch of epically good cheeses including the king of them all, Parmesan, and then a huge number of pleasant cheeses which are never going to set the world on fire. These are the ones that I use in my kitchen:

Ricotta: Sheer purity, ricotta is milky, soft and phenomenally useful. It's a leftovers cheese, made by heating up the whey left from making firmer cheeses, then skimming off the curds that rise to the top. Ricotta may be made from cow's, sheep's or goat's milk but the essential thing to remember is that this is an ultra-fresh cheese. Even when it comes out of a pasteurised sealed tub, it will only keep for a couple of days in the fridge. Its mildness is its superpower. Use it on bruschetta with tomatoes and basil, or whip it with sugar, vanilla and a spoonful or two of cream or yoghurt to eat with strawberries or slices of ripe peach. It's the basis of so many savoury fillings for ravioli and pies, makes a creamy sauce for pasta (page 240) and of course, it is the star of Italian baked cheesecakes (page 185).

Mozzarella: Needs no introduction. Buy cow's milk mozzarella (sold as *Fior di latte* in Italy) for everyday eating and cooking, cloud-soft buffalo mozzarella for best. A mozzarella-maker explained to me that Italians prefer their mozzarella firmer and chewy, while foreigners err towards softness. Either way, like ricotta it has a short shelf-life, just a couple of days. Burrata is mozzarella dressed up in Sunday finery, rich and a little decadent, Puglia's great gift to the world. Stracciatella is the inside bit of a burrata, shreds of mozzarella doused in cream.

Cacioricotta: A salty, hard white cheese that is much loved in Puglia. I can't say that I share this enthusiasm, but it is fine grated over a dish of *pasta al pomodoro*.

Caciocavallo: Shaped like a sagging money bag, *caciocavallo* is a cheese I've grown to appreciate. Young *caciocavallo* can be bland, but give it a bit of time to mature and it develops a satisfying tang. The best *caciocavallo* is made on a small scale in good dairies, then aged in natural caves. *Caciocavallo stagionato*, matured, melts really well – great for cheese on toast or in a dish of baked pasta.

Pecorino: Pecorino just means sheep's cheese and Italy has dozens if not hundreds of them. Broadly (very broadly) they fall into two categories: first, the young, mild, softer cheeses best eaten just as they are, or perhaps with a drizzle of honey and some walnuts; second, the hard, mature pecorinos meant for grating. They add a piquant, umami-laden saltiness to so many dishes in the south of Italy. When I list pecorino in the ingredients for a recipe, this is what I mean.

Parmesan: The king of all cheeses, umami god, bringer of life to the bland, Parmesan is hands down unbeatable in the kitchen. If you have any choice in the matter, choose Parmesan that has been matured for 30 months or more. It carries a heftier price tag, but you get such depth of flavour that it's worth it.

Grana Padano: Made in the same way as Parmesan, Grana Padano is always good, sometimes wonderful and is a perfectly reasonable alternative to Parmesan. As with Parmesan, the longer it has matured the richer the flavour.

Chillies

Southern Italian chillies are hot. Not Scotch Bonnet hot, but packing more of a fair mid-range punch. Red chillies are ubiquitous, fresh in the summer and dried in the winter. The aim is to give food a prickle of heat though no more than that. There are exceptions, of course, the most obvious being Calabria's world famous *'nduja* (page 218), which is made with three locally grown varieties.

Varieties invariably differ in intensity, but generally speaking, the classic cone-shaped red chillies sold by most British grocers are a little tamer but make an acceptable substitute.

Cotto di fichi

This thick syrup is made of nothing more than figs and water, boiled together then cooked down to a dark, caramelised fig essence. The naturally high sugar content means it keeps for months and months, ready to sweeten festival treats in the winter. It is bliss drizzled over ice cream or a bowl of thick yoghurt. If you can't get *cotto di fichi*, then North African date syrup makes a good substitute, or a dark honey.

Eggs

Recipes in this book have all been tested using medium eggs. This is a first for me. I've always bought large eggs, at least until I moved to Italy. The free-range eggs I get here are nearly always medium-sized. More importantly, I've also learned recently that it is painful for chickens to lay larger eggs, causing all sorts of problems which I won't go into here. This will come as no surprise to any woman who has given birth to a large baby. So please – buy free-range and medium. Above all, avoid extra-large eggs!

Flour

Italian flour is different to British flour and it's the bane of my life. The classification system is far more complex, with a troop of divisions, subdivisions and variables. So, to make my life simpler I tend to keep just three different Italian flours in my cupboard:

Grano Tenero 00 flour: Usually sold in the UK just as 00 flour. This is finely milled soft wheat flour, similar to plain flour but with a bit more body to it. It's great for making cakes, biscuits and egg pasta. However, most of the pasta down in the south is made with . . .

Semola rimacinata: This is a hard semolina flour, ground finely for pasta making and bread or pizza. It is essentially a finely ground version of old-fashioned pudding semolina, which is not a substitute. *Semola rimacinata* is mixed with hot water to make southern Italian pasta (in the past, eggs were way too expensive for most people). If you use it in bread-making, you will need to give it a long time to prove and develop its gluten. Sassy Italian delis may stock *semola rimacinata*, otherwise buy it online.

Farina di forza W350–W400: The equivalent of a strong white bread flour, this is the one I use for making fluffier, softer breads like the *picciddat* on page 191. The W number indicates the gluten percentage, the higher the better for baking bread.

Olive oil

Always, always extra virgin olive oil to get the proper, generous, Mediterranean flavour into your food. Most branded extra virgin olive oils have been blended for consistency. They are good for day-to-day cooking. Save a more expensive single estate olive oil for dressing salads and drizzling over bruschetta and the like.

Olive oil is absolutely fine for frying, despite what you may have read. It has a comparatively high smoking point which is well above the heat you'll need for frying food. I use sunflower oil for deep-frying largely because it is so much cheaper.

Pancetta

Salt-cured pork belly is a vital element in so many southern dishes. Pancetta *stesa* is cured in a single flat piece. I love it when it is *affumicata*, smoked. Although you can now buy ready-cut packs of pancetta *cubetti* or 'lardons', i.e. cut into cubes, you get a fuller, bolder flavour from a deli where they will cut you a thick slice from a whole slab of pancetta, for you to cube up at home. Either way, pancetta lardons breathe life and energy into the simplest sauces for pasta, or slow-cooked bean, vegetable or meat dishes. Thinly sliced pancetta is what you want for wrapping around chicken breasts or anything else that needs protecting and enhancing as it cooks.

High-quality pancetta, often *arrotolato*, rolled, can be savoured raw, thinly sliced alongside *prosciutto crudo* and other *salumi*.

Pasta

Southern Italian pasta is made with flour and water (recipe on page 228). No eggs. It's sturdier than the pasta from the north, but every bit as good in its own way. There are many, many different shapes, and every Italian will have firm and immovable opinions on which shape goes best with which sauce. These can differ from one side of a valley to the other. It all gets even more complicated when you factor in dry commercial pasta as well. As an outsider, I can see that the very small pasta shapes make sense for soup, cup-shaped pastas catch chunky sauces, but other than that I'm not so fussed.

The best dried pasta is made with bronze dies (as opposed to standard Teflon-coated dies), the perforated metal plates that are used to create the shapes. Sauces cling better to the rougher surface of bronze-cut pasta, so each mouthful is loaded with flavour. It's more costly but it's a small price worth paying.

Most important is the way you cook pasta:

1. Make sure you use a large saucepan – pasta needs room to move or else it coagulates into chewy lumps.

2. Ideally, you'll heat 1 litre of water and 10g of salt for each 100g of uncooked pasta.

3. Use a timer! Cook pasta for a minute or two less than advised on the packet and drain when it is still just a shade more al dente than you like it, but before you drain it . . .

4. . . . scoop out a mugful of the cooking water and reserve.

5. Heat the sauce in a wide, deep frying pan, then tip the drained pasta into the sauce. Toss over a moderate heat, adding slurps of the reserved pasta water. Why? Because the starch in the pasta water gifts a silkiness to any sauce, helping it to coat the pasta evenly, carrying flavours right into the pasta itself. By the time everything is perfectly mixed and sizzling hot, the pasta will be perfectly cooked.

Peppers

This is really a note for anyone who may be cooking from this book while in Italy. As you will have realised, Italian peppers are vast compared to the bell peppers that are available in the UK. So in a recipe that calls for 1 pepper, half an Italian pepper will be all that you need. And while we are on this subject . . .

. . . *Peperoni* means pepper, as in red, green or yellow bell pepper or capsicum. It is not a sausage.

Salsiccia

These are fresh sausages and there are many of them, eaten grilled or fried, or crumbled into sauces for pasta, particularly in Basilicata and Calabria. Italian sausages are usually made of pure meat, fat and lean, with seasonings but no breadcrumbs or rusk. This gives a firmer texture and a meatier flavour. When buying sausages for an Italian recipe, choose the best pork sausage you can find, with a high percentage of meat. Southern sausages are often flavoured with fennel, wine, or sweet or hot paprika, so it's perfectly reasonable to add an extra spoonful of any of these to the pan with your plain pork sausage.

Salsiccia al punto di coltello, literally tip of the knife sausage, is a coarse-textured hand-chopped pure pork sausage.

Tomatoes

One of the biggest culinary surprises in the south of Italy is the way they use tomatoes. Throughout much of the year the main cooking tomato is the cherry tomato, mostly used in relatively small quantities as a seasoning rather than as the foundation of a tomato sauce. In mid-summer, many families still cook up larger red-ripe juicy tomatoes in vast quantities to make a fine store of passata, puréed cooked tomatoes, for the cooler months. Everyone else buys ready-made passata in the supermarket. For salads, it's the slightly underripe, green-red tomato that is preferred for its crispness and its sweet-sharp herbal flavour.

Tinned tomatoes: Don't buy cheap tinned tomatoes. This is not a quality issue, though it's true that cheaper tins may contain fewer tomatoes and more juice. This is a question of morality. In too many Italian establishments, migrant tomato pickers are working in conditions that are tantamount to slavery. Housed in tin shacks, with little in the way of sanitation, this is a national scandal. In theory there are regulations to prevent this but they are easily circumnavigated. Bigger international brands are not all squeaky clean, but they are a better bet.

Puglia

A Prediction

A few years ago an acquaintance declared that she was now a futurologist. I was impressed at her chutzpah. Predicting the future, even based on extensive knowledge of the present and the past in any particular field, is a risky business. Not only do you have to be self-confident and bold enough to hoist your opinions up the flagpole, you must also be humble enough to accept mistakes or at least thick-skinned enough to shrug them off when the world doesn't progress in the way you promised it would.

For all that, I am prepared to predict that over the next few years *cime di rapa* will go mainstream. For now, this beloved southern Italian leafy green is a bit of a smug secret outside of its home territory. In Puglia it is a cold-weather essential, cooked with pasta in virtually every family kitchen from top to bottom (there's a recipe for Orecchiette alle Cime di Rapa in my previous book, *A Curious Absence of Chickens*). It appears as a *contorno*, a side dish, simply boiled for a few minutes, then sautéd with olive oil and garlic or braised slowly with white wine. The fondness for this mildly bitter, sprouting broccoli relative reaches out into Basilicata and Calabria. These days you can find jars of preserved *cime di rapa sott'olio* or *cime*-speckled *taralli* and dried pasta. Smarter *pizzerie* serve up delicious pizzas moistened with *cime* purée in place of tomato sauce.

The good news is that it grows easily and vigorously in more northerly climates. Smart greengrocers are beginning to stock it in the UK and in the States, and trendy restaurants are sliding it into their menus. The biggest stumbling block is the name. Oddly, it usually gets translated as 'turnip tops', though it isn't actually the top of any turnip. The turnip greens eaten in southern American states are similar but don't taste the same. Better to opt for the Italian variants, of which there are plenty to go round – so *cime di rapa*, or *friarielli* (the Neapolitan name) or *rapini* (Tuscany). Search it out now; get ahead of the game. I predict that it will be worth your while.

Preparing *cime di rapa*

Cime di rapa needs to be totally, utterly, squeakily fresh. If the leaves look floppy and tired, if the little florets are yellowing, if there is the odd slimy patch, they are not fresh so don't buy them. Like so many leafy greens, they can be gritty especially when the weather is wet, so the first thing to do is to rinse them thoroughly in a basin of cold water. Swish them around a little, then stand back for a few seconds and let the grit settle before scooping the *cime* out. If there has been torrential rain around recently, splashing more mud up on to the leaves, you may need to give them a second rinse in fresh water. Then let them drain in a colander.

Trim off the thickest, tough stems and discard. Throw out damaged leaves as well. If you are not using them immediately, wrap loosely in kitchen paper and pop into a plastic bag. Knot the ends and store in the fridge for no more than a day or two. Longer than this and they will lose their freshest flavour and begin to whiff of the sulphurous scent of old brassicas.

Cime di Rapa 'Nfucate

Braised Cime di Rapa with Chilli and White Wine

It's no good rushing a good thing. This method of slowly braising *cime di rapa* (or purple sprouting broccoli, for that matter) is definitely a good thing, bringing out the deepest, greenest, most rounded of flavours. I'd happily eat it on its own, with a thick slice of good bread to mop up the juices. More conventionally, serve it alongside a plate of grilled sausages or with lamb or pork.

Serves 4

500g *cime di rapa*, or purple sprouting broccoli, cleaned and trimmed
3 tablespoons extra virgin olive oil, plus extra to finish
2 cloves of garlic, thinly sliced
1 medium-hot red chilli, fresh or dried, finely chopped
150ml dry white wine
salt

Pile the *cime* up on the chopping board and slash roughly.

Spoon the olive oil into a deep frying pan large enough to squeeze in all the *cime di rapa*. Add the garlic and the chilli and warm over a moderate heat until the garlic begins to sizzle. Pile in the *cime di rapa*, add 100ml of water and the wine, and season with salt. Turn the *rapa* so that everything is nicely mixed together, then clamp on the lid and cook gently for 45–50 minutes. I know this seems like a ridiculously long time to cook fresh leafy greens, but stay with it. Check them occasionally, give them a stir, and if necessary add a splash more water.

Ultimately you are aiming for a delectable tenderness of greens with the lightest slick of cooking liquid left in the bottom of the pan. Taste and add more salt as needed. Pile into a serving dish and drizzle over a thread of fresh olive oil.

Cime di Rapa e Capperi in Pastella

Cime di Rapa and Caper Fritters

My neighbour Maria introduced me to *cime di rapa* fritters one autumn afternoon, hot from the pan, the batter swaddling the cluster of leaves, somehow emphasising their unique fragrance.

Serves 6

300g *cime di rapa*, cleaned and trimmed
2 tablespoons capers, rinsed thoroughly if salted
50g freshly grated Pecorino or Parmesan
sunflower oil, for deep-frying

For the batter
200g plain flour
1 teaspoon baking powder
½ teaspoon salt
250ml chilled sparkling water

Put a pan of salted water on to boil. Pile the *cime di rapa* on your chopping board and shred coarsely. Blanch for 4 minutes in boiling water, then drain well.

Put a pan of sunflower oil on to heat up. Put the flour into a bowl with the baking powder and salt. Gradually whisk in the sparkling water. Stir in the *cime di rapa*, capers and grated cheese. Slide well-charged dessertspoonfuls of the mixture into the hot oil – don't overcrowd the pan. Fry for around 4 minutes, until golden brown. Drain on kitchen paper. Season with a little extra salt, then eat while still warm and crisp.

Just a Little Fillet o' Fish, Per Favore

We get superlative fish in Puglia. No surprise there, what with the long, long coastline. The heel of Italy is embraced by its two seas, the Adriatic looking out towards Albania and Greece to the east, the Ionian to the west, nestling comfortably into the boot's instep. Heading off to the coast for a slap-up plate or three of freshest seafood is a regular family treat. It's a joy to peer over at a table crowded with grandparents, parents and gaggles of children, all tucking into *pesce crudo* (raw fish), spiny black sea urchins, or a heap of *fritto misto* (deep-fried morsels of squid, octopus and little fish), glistening grilled *orata* (sea bream) or tender-as-butter octopus stew.

The one fishy thing that you rarely see is a humble fillet. The story is the same, I discover, as I travel along the Ionian coast towards Reggio Calabria. When I ask my sage, knowledgeable fishmonger, Tonino, to fillet the fish I'm buying for clients, he looks disapproving. '*Perché?*' he asks. 'Why? The sweetest flesh is closest to the bone. Filleting wastes so much.' He's absolutely right, of course. So I blame it on fussy foreigners who know no better, not liking to admit that occasionally I, too, crave the easy eating fish fillet in place of the juicier, tastier, bonier whole fish.

Tonino, with a discernible lack of enthusiasm, passes the filleting on to his assistant. The result is variable, but rarely a fillet as I know it. The head is cleaved in two but still attached to the flesh, another display of cultural diversity. There may still be fins or tail clinging on, the bones of the ribcage still lurk below the surface. The squeamishness of foreigners is a mystery to an Italian who expects to see a whole fish on his plate.

The exception to this rule is anchovies. Tonino and his co-workers have no qualms about filleting mountains of silvery anchovies for their clients. They work fast, slitting open the stomach with a deft finger, tugging out innards, spine and with them the head too. Within a few minutes they are packed neatly into small tubs, ready to go.

Alici, Orata o Spigola Arracanate

Roast Anchovy, Sea Bream or Sea Bass Fillets with Breadcrumbs, Mint and Capers

This is a dish from Puglia's west coast, first tasted in a popular backstreet Taranto restaurant as part of an *antipasto di mare*, a feast of small seafood dishes to whet the appetite. There it was a brace of mouthfuls of anchovy, topped with crisp crumbs. Now I make it at home as a main course, a quick dinner, with sea bream or sea bass fillets. It's delicious but please don't tell Tonino.

**Serves 6 as a starter when made with anchovies,
2 as a main course when made with sea bass or bream**

400g fresh anchovies, filleted (see page 27), or 4 fillets of
    sea bream or sea bass (400–500g total weight)
extra virgin olive oil
2 tablespoons dry white wine
salt and freshly ground black pepper
75g fresh or stale bread
1 clove of garlic, roughly chopped
1 teaspoon dried oregano
the leaves from 2 sprigs of mint
2 tablespoons capers, rinsed thoroughly if salted

To serve
wedges of lemon

Preheat the oven to 250°C/230°C fan/gas 9. Check your fish fillets and trim out any small bones or lingering fish scales. Oil an ovenproof dish and lay in the fish fillets, skin side down.

Drizzle over the white wine, then season with salt and freshly ground black pepper.

Process the bread with the garlic, oregano, mint and 2 tablespoons of olive oil. Stir in the capers, then sprinkle over the fish. Bake for 10–12 minutes, and whip out of the oven as soon as the breadcrumbs are nicely browned. Tuck a few wedges of lemon alongside and serve.

Alici Marinate

Marinated Anchovies

This simplest of recipes is indisputably the ultimate way to eat fresh anchovies. So, so utterly delicious. So, so, so easy. The trickiest part is finding the anchovies themselves. With their soft, oil-rich flesh they don't have much of a shelf-life. Get them home, marinate them straight away and then relax. They'll keep in the fridge for 3 or 4 days.

Serves 4–6

300g fresh anchovies, cleaned and filleted (see opposite)
juice of 2 lemons
2 cloves of garlic, finely chopped
1 fresh red chilli, deseeded and finely chopped
salt and freshly ground black pepper
3–4 tablespoons extra virgin olive oil
1 tablespoon finely chopped parsley

Check over your anchovy fillets and pinch off the tails if they are still there and any lingering tips of the spine. Put into a bowl and add the lemon juice, half the garlic, half the chilli, salt and freshly ground black pepper. Mix delicately with your fingers, then cover and leave to marinate in the fridge for at least 1 hour and up to 24 hours.

Transfer the fillets carefully to a serving dish, leaving the murky juices behind. Drizzle with olive oil, then scatter over the remaining garlic and chilli and the parsley. Serve cold or at room temperature.

How to clean and fillet an anchovy

When you don't have an amiable fishmonger to fillet anchovies for you, this is how you go about the task. You don't even need a knife. Pick up an anchovy in one hand, then grasp the head and pinch it off, bringing some of the innards with it. With your thumb, open up the fish flat. Gently pull the spine away from the flesh and discard. Pinch off the tail. Once they are all done, rinse them under the cold tap, pat dry gently with kitchen paper and you're good to go.

Casarecce al Sughetto di Pesce

Casarecce Pasta with a Little Tomato and Fish Sauce

Despite Tonino's dismay at my request for fillets of fish, he makes sure I take the bones and heads away with me, insisting that I use them to make a *sughetto di pesce*, a little sauce, for my pasta. Don't waste all that fish that you've paid for anyway, he insists. It is excellent advice. There is a surprising amount of flesh left on the naked bones, plenty to flavour the sauce as long as you are prepared to spend a little time picking it off.

Serves 4

fish bones and head from 1 medium-sized bream (from
      a 550–600g whole fish) or sea bass, or 1 fillet of fish
1 bay leaf
the stems only of 2 sprigs of parsley
1 sprig of thyme
2 tablespoons extra virgin olive oil
1 onion, chopped
3 cloves of garlic, chopped
2 tablespoons finely chopped parsley
400ml passata
salt and freshly ground black pepper
350–400g dried *casarecce*, *cavatelli* or *penne*
to garnish: a little extra chopped parsley

Put the bones and head or fillet of fish into a saucepan with the bay leaf, parsley stems and thyme. Add water to just cover. Bring up to the boil, then reduce the heat to a lazy simmer. Cook for 10 minutes. Leave until cool enough to handle. Flake as much fish as you can from the bones and head, or rip the fillet apart into small pieces with two forks. Strain the stock and reserve.

Put the olive oil into a frying pan and add the onion and garlic. Place over a moderate heat and fry gently for around 10 minutes, without browning. Stir in the parsley, then pour in the passata and 300ml of the fish stock. Season with salt and freshly ground black pepper. Simmer gently for 15 minutes. Taste and adjust the seasoning. Stir in the flaked fish and simmer for another minute.

Meanwhile, bring a large pan of well-salted water up to the boil. Add the pasta and cook until just al dente. Drain and toss with the sauce. Sprinkle a little parsley over the top and serve immediately.

Exploding Tomatoes on Toast

Ostuni's main car park lounges at the foot of the beautiful white town. Most visitors park up wherever they can find a space (in the summer months, when the town is overrun with tourists, Italian creative parking is brilliantly in evidence), look up to the town's white walls above them and trudge uphill to the town centre. If they turned around their gaze would fall upon the strange sight of a huge domed church, isolated in the centre of a verdant market garden. This is the Santuario Madonna della Grata, built over the remains of a fourth-century BC Messapian necropolis.

Grata translates literally as a grate or a lattice, but in this particular spot, this particular sanctuary, it means the human spine and ribcage. Centuries ago, a local farmer who suffered excruciating back pains prayed to the Madonna to help him. She did and he returned joyfully to his work, perhaps in these fields that still surround the building. The terraces of the Giardini della Grata have been a source of food for Ostuni since medieval times, when agricultural workers transformed the stone tombs of the ancient tribe into water cisterns and vegetable patches. Post-war the Giardini were abandoned – impossible to work with modern tractors and farming equipment – and left to run wild.

Now it has been transformed back into glorious productivity. The Bio Solequo Cooperative works with the original terraces and around the cisterns and ditches, planting long curved rows of ancient varieties of tomatoes and many other imperilled strains of Puglian vegetables. It is a small paradise shaded with fig trees and prickly pears, displayed for all to see from the walls of the white city.

Oddly, I first met Antonio Capriglia, Solequo's president, in the non-verdant tourist office one cool autumn evening. He presided over a brace of small trestle tables laden from edge to edge with some thirty different varieties of cherry tomato, maybe more. I lost count. Over the years he has collected over 100 identifiably diverse variations on Puglia's favourite cooking tomato. Red, yellow, orange, purple, green, beige, round, oval, pear-shaped, comparatively big and comparatively small, the permutations are giddying. For all their myriad minor features, the big division here is between summer tomatoes and winter tomatoes.

Winter tomatoes, though they ripen in July and August, will keep right through the autumn and winter. Yup, no need for drying or canning or freezing or high-tech gas-filled chillers. Winter tomatoes need no more than relatively dry, airy, cool conditions to survive intact and edible. Remarkable. Top of the winter tomato pops is the Regina tomato, which earns its name, or rather her name (Regina means queen) from the way the green tips of the calyx curl regally up and inwards like a crown. It also clings relatively firmly to the fruit and that turns out to be a big bonus.

Antonio's partner Renza shows me how the tomatoes are strung together in bunches like oversized red grapes. She deftly twists cotton thread around the base of the calyxes linking seven small rosy Reginas together, seven per skein because she likes the number seven. She loads the skeins on to a length of strong hemp rope, knotting the ends together every now and again. Then there it is, a magnificent *ramasole*, hefty and gleaming in the summer sun. Renza reckons it weighs in at some 4–5 kilos of little tomatoes that will keep right through to next spring if they aren't eaten along the way.

It's one of those odd little life quirks that you can remain totally ignorant of a word or a song or a recipe or whatever it is that clicks your brain cells into recognition until one day it pings on to your radar for the first time, then suddenly it is everywhere. I've spent a large chunk of the last four years researching local dishes, never once spotting a reference to the simple joy of exploding tomatoes. Until the day I watched Renza stringing her winter tomatoes in the fields of the Giardini della Grata beneath Ostuni's white walls. Since then they keep popping up with unprecedented regularity, in a Lecce restaurant, in a comment below a recipe online, in a little pamphlet of recipes from the south of the Salento region.

Antonio cooked *pomodorini scattariciati* right there and then in the field, pan perched on an alarmingly wobbly gas burner. It's a recipe for when there's nothing much else to hand, just olive oil, tomatoes, garlic and chillies and a little bread or pasta, the basics of every Puglian kitchen. Inevitably there are variations on the theme: in the Trattoria delle Due Archi they add onions, some recipes call for capers or olives, here there is a handful of basil, there mint or parsley.

Scattariciati is a dialect word and we come to the conclusion, via a mix of my limited Italian and Antonio and Renza's limited English, that it translates as 'exploded'. Further research is pointing to the less dramatic 'burst'. Too prosaic. I like to think of those taut-skinned little orbs building up so much trapped juicy steam that they explode their goodness into the pan.

Pomodorini Scattariciati

Exploding Tomatoes

This is one of the simplest recipes in this book and one of the tastiest things I've eaten in a long time. You will need a frying pan with a lid to contain all those exploding saucy little tomatoes. Do not stint on the olive oil – 5 tablespoons absolute minimum.

If you are happy with a casual kitchen supper approach, put the pan of cooked tomatoes on the table, arm everyone with thick slices of good bread and let them scoop the gloop straight out of the pan. If that's just too informal, smear the burst tomatoes thickly on to the slices of bread and serve on plates. For a more substantial supper, toss the burst tomatoes with freshly cooked pasta and a handful of basil leaves.

Serves 3–4

5–6 tablespoons extra virgin olive oil
3 cloves of garlic, peeled and each cut into 3
2 fresh red chillies, sliced
2 bay leaves
500g cherry tomatoes
1 teaspoon dried oregano
salt and freshly ground black pepper

To serve
thick slices of good bread or toast, or hot pasta

Put a heavy-based frying pan over a high heat. Add the oil, garlic, chillies and bay leaves. Let it all heat up and start to sizzle – give it a good minute or two, then carefully tip in the tomatoes. Clamp on the lid and shake gently over the heat. It takes a few minutes for them to build up a good head of steam, then they will start to split open.

Give them a good stir, crushing the split tomatoes gently, then cover again and cook for a few more minutes. Repeat. Take off the lid, add the oregano, stir, and roughly crush down the remaining tomatoes to make a thick, chunky sauce. Season with salt and freshly ground black pepper. Serve warm or at room temperature, smeared thickly on slices of bread or toast, or tossed into hot pasta.

Cicerchie e Ceci Neri al Pomodoro

Puglian Beans in Red Wine Tomato Sauce

From Puglia's Murgia region come these two unusual pulses. *Cicerchie* are small, grey-beige dried peas that look like semi-deflated balloons. They have a nutty, almost grassy taste. You can buy them relatively easily in other countries but only from specialist suppliers. To get something of the grassy pea flavour you can replace them with split yellow peas. Unlike *cicerchie*, split peas do not need to be soaked before cooking.

Ceci neri are black chickpeas. Smaller and wrinklier than your average chickpea, they taste similar but meatier. They are very tough to track down outside of Italy, as production is almost exclusive to this one area. Curiously, however, you also find black chickpeas (*kala chana*) in India and hence in Indian produce shops. They're not quite the same, a little smaller still than the Italian black chickpea, but a fine substitute.

Serves 4–6

80g *cicerchie*, soaked overnight, or 80g dried split
    yellow peas
80g *ceci neri* or *kala chana*, soaked overnight
salt and freshly ground black pepper
3 tablespoons extra virgin olive oil
1 onion, chopped
3 cloves of garlic, chopped
1 red chilli, chopped
1 teaspoon fennel seeds
100ml red wine
1 x 400g tin of chopped tomatoes
2 heaped tablespoons tomato purée

a handful of basil leaves
½ teaspoon caster sugar, if needed
to garnish: a few basil leaves

Drain the *cicerchie* and *ceci neri*. Cook in separate saucepans, covered plentifully with water and with a few pinches of salt. Skim off any scum that rises to the surface, then reduce the heat to a gentle simmer. Cook until tender. Cooking times vary considerably. Split peas are quick off the mark and should be soft but still with a slight firmness after 35–50 minutes. *Cicerchie*, *ceci neri* and *kala chana usually* take longer – start checking them after around 30 minutes, but be prepared for them to take anything up to an hour and a half to soften. Once they're cooked, drain and run them under the cold tap.

Meanwhile, put the olive oil, onion, garlic and chilli into a saucepan and set over a gentle heat. Fry slowly until the onion is golden and soft. Add the fennel seeds and cook for a couple more minutes, then tip in the red wine. Boil for another minute or so, then add the tomatoes, tomato purée and around half the basil leaves. Add 200ml of water, too. Simmer for 20–30 minutes, until thick and fragrant. Taste and adjust the seasoning, adding a little sugar if it is too tart. Stir in the *cicerchie* and *ceci neri* and simmer everything together for 3 or 4 minutes more, to heat through. Stir in the last of the basil leaves. Serve hot or warm, garnished with a few more basil leaves.

A King of the Funghi

Cardoncelli are mushrooms of substance. They once grew abundantly on the plains of the Murgia plateau which spans the north of Puglia and the east of Basilicata. Here the wild *cardoncelli* that sprang up after late summer and autumn storms were poetically known as the 'sons of thunder'. These days they are rare and protected.

The handsome town of Altamura, in the Alta Murgia, is best known for its excellent, golden-crumbed bread, cooked in ancient wood-fired ovens. It's also where *cardoncelli* were first successfully cultivated back in the 1970s. Now they are a staple sold in every supermarket around the region.

Their flesh is firm, mildly scented with a soft mushroom breeze when raw. This is transformed into a satisfying umami-imbued meatiness once cooked. They are sooooo much nicer than their cousins, the plain, damp oyster mushrooms. In the UK, they are sold as king oyster mushrooms and they are definitely aristocrats in the world of commercially grown fungi.

The stem is the thing with *cardoncelli*. It is broad and sturdy, topped with a teensy grey-brown cap when young, spreading to a wider brown-gilled umbrella as it matures. Preparation is minimal. Slice off the base, wipe away any traces of grit with a damp cloth, then slice the stems thickly. As with all mushrooms, do not douse them in water. They soak it up like a sponge, then it leaches out in the pan in a dismal puddle.

Insalata di Cardoncelli e Borlotti

King Oyster Mushroom and Borlotti Bean Salad

Mushrooms and beans work so well together – a happy blend of gently contrasting textures and flavours. In this salad, there's a hint of sweetness from the fig (or date or pomegranate) syrup and the brightness of whole parsley leaves as well.

Serves 6

4–6 tablespoons extra virgin olive oil
500g king oyster mushrooms, cleaned and thickly sliced
2 cloves of garlic, finely chopped
1 x 400g tin of borlotti beans, drained and rinsed
¼ of a red onion, finely chopped
1 tablespoon red wine vinegar
a dash of lemon juice
1 tablespoon *cotto di fichi* (fig syrup) or date molasses or pomegranate molasses
salt and freshly ground black pepper
a good handful of whole parsley leaves

Heat 3 tablespoons of olive oil over a high heat. When it is really hot, add half the mushroom slices, spreading them out in a single layer. Fry until golden brown underneath, then turn and fry the other sides. Transfer to a bowl. Repeat with the remaining mushroom slices, adding more oil as needed. Once they are browned on both sides, add the garlic to the pan, mix, and fry for another 30 seconds or so just to take the raw edge away. Scoop the mushrooms, garlic and oil out into the bowl. Add all the remaining ingredients except the parsley leaves. Mix, then taste and adjust the seasoning. Once the mushrooms are completely cool, toss in the parsley leaves.

Cardoncelli Trifolati

Fried King Oyster Mushrooms with Parsley, Wine and Garlic

Trifolati is usually translated as 'sautéd' but while succinct, that's only half the story. Cubes or slices of raw food are indeed sautéd in olive oil over a high heat, but the essential difference is that they are then finished with parsley and garlic. In this particular recipe, there's an additional hit of chilli and a glug or two of white wine. Mushrooms, aubergines and courgettes can all be *trifolati*.

Cardoncelli trifolati are good as a side dish, but for a more substantial meal, toss with hot pasta or pile high on thick griddled bread.

Serves 4

4 tablespoons extra virgin olive oil
400g king oyster mushrooms, cleaned and thickly sliced
1 red chilli, finely chopped
2 cloves of garlic, finely chopped
3 tablespoons dry white wine
salt and freshly ground black pepper
1 tablespoon roughly chopped parsley

Heat 3 tablespoons of olive oil over a high heat. When it is really hot, add half the mushroom slices, spreading them out in a single layer. Fry until golden brown underneath, then turn and fry the other side. Transfer to a bowl. Repeat with the remaining mushroom slices, adding the rest of the oil. Once they are browned on both sides, add the chilli and garlic to the pan, mix, and fry for another 30 seconds or so just to take the raw edge away.

Quickly tip the first batch of mushrooms back into the pan. Add the wine, salt and freshly ground black pepper. Stir the mush-rooms around in it, then let it boil off for a few seconds until almost all evaporated. Toss in the parsley, taste and adjust the seasoning and serve hot.

Zucchine alla Poverella

Fried Courgette, Mint and Lemon Salad

This is a recipe that has spawned its own fan club, a recipe that has converted those who believed courgettes a waste of time, a recipe with just a handful of easy ingredients, a recipe for anyone who grows their own courgettes and is constantly searching for new things to do with them. We usually include it in our selection of *antipasti* when we are cooking for clients, who more often than not pick it out as the best of a splendid bunch. What we don't do is make it for large groups, because it demands dedication and time. I've learnt from experience that there is no rushing *zucchine alla poverella*. First of all, you absolutely must salt the thin green-white slices for half an hour or more. Skip this and you will end up with mush in the pan. Second, you absolutely must dry the slices properly on layers of kitchen paper or tea towels. Again, if you don't you risk mush. Third, you absolutely must fry the courgettes in batches so that each slice is browned on both sides to the point of crispness. None of this is difficult, but it takes time and attention to detail.

Serves 4

3 medium-sized courgettes
salt and freshly ground black pepper
4–5 tablespoons extra virgin olive oil
1 large or 2 small cloves of garlic, finely chopped
juice of ½–1 lemon
a good handful of fresh mint leaves, plus a few extra to
    garnish

Slice the courgettes as thinly as you can, then pile them into a colander set over a plate or bowl and sprinkle them with salt. Mix and leave to drain for at least half an hour. Pat dry on clean tea towels or kitchen paper.

Heat the olive oil in a wide frying pan. Add a single layer of courgette slices and fry over a brisk heat, turning once or twice until well browned. As they brown, scoop them out into a bowl. Replace the browned courgette slices with more uncooked slices, and keep going, patiently, until all your courgettes are richly browned. Just as the last ones are nearly finished, throw in the garlic and let it sizzle for a few seconds. Scrape everything out into the bowl. Add the lemon juice, ripped up mint leaves and freshly ground black pepper. Mix and taste. If it isn't totally delicious, you probably need to add a little salt or more lemon or both. Serve at room temperature, with a few fresh mint leaves scattered over.

Lampascioni

In the early twentieth century, Basilicata had one essential commodity that Puglia lacked. Water. Or rather, relatively easily accessible, usable water. Puglia is blessed with its 500 miles of coastline, but freshwater rivers it has virtually none. Beneath its surface, green for a few months in winter and spring, red-brown and parched for the rest of the year, the tufa rock is riddled with caves, carved out over millennia by slushing, swishing, permeating water that has settled underground. Occasionally you see and hear incongruously large hulks of machinery, dwarfing a pretty gaggle of *trulli* or farm buildings in the middle of nowhere, drilling down hundreds of metres through the rock to the hidden water reserves below. Well construction is tough enough now, but it must have been hellish hard in past centuries.

Eventually, into this waterless breach, rode the Aquedotto Pugliesi to the rescue. In the early years of the twentieth century, the company laid down a phenomenal network of pipes, bringing water from Basilicata and Campania's springs, lakes and dams right the way down to Puglia's tip some 400 kilometres away, branching out here, there and almost everywhere to towns and villages throughout the dry and dusty heel. A phenomenal feat of engineering and determination. Key to the whole operation were the beautiful pumping stations, painted the characteristic rust-red and housing gleaming metal state-of-the-art steam pumps.

The Villa Castelli pumping station rises up among the olive trees. Occasionally its doors are opened up to the public. We visited one perfect warm spring day, marvelling at the burnished engineering, then strolled up the broad path over the hidden pipeline towards the town. On either side of us meadows and orchards were filled with spring flowers and a scattering of wild strawberries. Red, white, yellow, orange and the ubiquitous blue of the wild tassel hyacinth (*Muscari racemosum*), relative of the spring grape hyacinths that British gardeners plant alongside crocuses for early colour. These resilient bulbs, *lampascioni*, are embedded deep down in the stony soil, waiting for spring rains to send up tell-tale shoots.

What seemed surprising to me was that there were any left to bloom at all. Their bulbs are a highly prized vegetable here in Puglia, Basilicata and to an extent in Calabria, sold by the kilo from muddy crates. To the uninitiated they look like a messy tangle of dirty little shallots; to a southern cook and her family, a beloved cold weather treat. They are, I think it fair to say, an acquired taste – bitter, a touch slippery like okra, not really oniony at all.

I'd conjured up an image of enterprising locals out in the wilds, digging up bulb after bulb in the chill of the winter months. Then, at the market last week, I happened to glance at the label on a crate of *lampascioni* as I passed by. Ha! Not nearly as local as most people think – these ones were imported from Tunisia. In the supermarket, the punnets of dirt-encrusted bulbs hailed from Algeria. Morocco is also an exporter, sending them not only to Italy but also to Greece, another committed land of muscari-eaters, and more surprisingly to America – no idea who's doing what with them there. It's a trade that has been going on for at least eighty years and probably far longer. Thank you, North Africa, for saving those lovely splashes of blue in Puglia's spring fields. Sorry if yours are in decline.

Lampascioni bulbs are used in any number of ways, preserved in olive oil to serve with sliced cured meats and cheeses at the start of a meal, boiled and scrambled with eggs and greens, in salads, in slow braised stews of lamb or pork and, best of all (I think, as do many who come to them as outsiders), deep-fried into crisp-petalled morsels for the *antipasto* spread.

This, to my mind, is the best *lampascioni* entry portal for the uninitiated. Next, move on to Calabrese-style sweet-sour *lampascioni*, which go so well with cheeses and cured meats, or with a grilled pork chop.

Preparing lampascioni

Lampascioni are always generously encrusted with dirt – as you wash them clean, one by one, console yourself that this means they come from somewhere that is not highly mechanised, that they haven't already been through a pile of processing and that they will probably taste all the better for it. My mum always used to insist that mucky potatoes or carrots were superior to those that had been mechanically cleaned, and I like to think that the same applies to *lampascioni*.

Once clean, slice a paper-thin disc off the base of each one, slice off the tip, then peel/rub away the dry outer skin. Soak in cold water for at least 2 hours, changing the water once or twice if you remember. This draws out some of their bitterness.

Lampascioni Fritti

Deep-Fried Lampascioni Flowers

Make these as part of an *antipasto* starter spread, or as a starter in their own right, perched on a small salad of rocket, halved cherry tomatoes and toasted hazelnuts, dressed with red wine vinegar and olive oil.

Per person

3 or 4 *lampascioni*, cleaned and soaked in cold water for
  at least 2 hours
sunflower oil, for deep-frying
salt

Drain the *lampascioni* and dry on kitchen paper. Cut each one almost into 6 wedges, stopping the blade a few millimetres from the base, so they stay together. To do this without stress, line up something thin and hard (like the lid of a jam jar) on the chopping board next to the bulb, to prevent the knife cutting right through to the board.

Heat a 4cm depth of sunflower oil to around 180–190°C (or until a small cube of bread browns in 30–40 seconds). Carefully lower in the prepared *lampascioni* and cook for 3–4 minutes, until they have opened out and the 'petals' are crisply browned. Drain for a minute or two on kitchen paper, sprinkle with salt and serve while still hot.

Lampascioni in Agrodolce

Calabrese-Style Sweet and Sour Lampascioni

Sweet and sour and a little bitter, think of this as the Negroni of the vegetable firmament, to be sipped rather than glugged. Serve at room temperature with cheese and cured meats, or gently warmed to accompany rich meats like pork or duck.

Serves 4

300g *lampascioni*, cleaned and soaked in water for at least 2 hours
1 tablespoon extra virgin olive oil
2 tablespoons red wine vinegar
1 tablespoon sugar
1 medium hot fresh red chilli, finely chopped
salt

Bring a large pan of salted water to the boil. Tip in the *lampascioni*, bring back to the boil, then simmer until just tender but with a slight firmness at the centre – 8–10 minutes. Drain.

Heat the olive oil in a frying pan or saucepan. Add the *lampascioni* and cook over a high heat until they are beginning to brown here and there. Swiftly add the vinegar, sugar, chilli and salt. Cook for another 3–4 minutes, stirring frequently, until the vinegar and sugar have fused and cooked down to coat the *lampascioni* in a sticky essence. Draw off the heat and serve warm or cold.

It's Grano, not Grana, Stupid!

Learning a foreign language is awash with pitfalls. Some funny, some hugely misleading, some rude and others just frustrating. Some of the small technical differences I have, I think, now mastered. Undoubtedly there are far more that I haven't. I just hope my mistakes do no more than amuse Italian acquaintances. It's innocent enough to imagine that the word *fattoria*, for instance, means factory. It doesn't. It means a farm. Both the jewellers and the confectioner's a few streets away have doors leading to their *laboratori*. Not a sterile room full of test tubes, petri dishes and microscopes. It's their work-shop, the place where they make what they sell. No Italian home cook will extend the shelf-life of their jams and jellies by adding *preservativi*. Condoms in the *marmellata*? No. No. No. I've learnt too that I should absolutely and totally never ever tell a new mother that I am excited, *eccitata,* to meet her newborn child. Why? Because *eccitato* means horny.

Less offensive is the not-so-simple difference between *grano* and *grana.* Type either into Deepl, Reverso or Google Translate and both yield the word 'grain'. Helpfully, wheat pops up for *grano.* Both are also slang for 'money'. Faced with the words on a menu, this is really not at all helpful. It took me a while to suss that they are not used interchangeably when it comes to actual cooking and eating. Context, context, context. A pizza with *grana* on it comes embellished with *grana* cheese – hard, granular, mature cheese, most probably Parmesan or its neighbour Grana Padano.

If it is *grano con ragù* or *insalata di grano*, what you will get on your plate is a heap of cooked wheat berries.

The Tavoliere delle Puglie in the north of the region was transformed from grazing land to wheatfields post Italy's uni-fication and is still one of the country's main wheat-growing areas. Pockets of wheat grow along the flatter southern coastal areas of Basilicata and Calabria, too. I guess that in the past grains of wheat were more readily accessible than the rice grown in the wetter north of Italy. Today they are still served once in a while with stews or as the basis of a salad or as a pudding. What surprises me most about this is that we don't all tuck into whole wheat grains regularly. I love the nubbly, soft chewiness of them, blessed with a nutty, grainy character that welcomes all manner of more dominant flavours.

How to cook whole wheat, farro (emmer) or spelt grains

Whole wheat berries or kernels come in a multitude of forms but they all belong to the genus *Triticum*. The bag of ordinary flour in your cupboard will be *Triticum aestivum*. Most Italian pasta is made with durum wheat flour, *Triticum durum*. When it comes to whole grains, the easiest ones to track down (some supermarkets, whole food and health food shops or online) are standard wheat berries (*T. aestivum*), or emmer, often sold under its Italian name, *farro* (*T. dicoccum*), or spelt (*T. spelta*).

Thank heavens that in the kitchen you don't need to worry too much about which one you are using. They all cook in much the same way and the tastes are similar enough for them to be interchangeable in recipes. Farro and spelt may be more digestible for those with minor gluten allergies, but if that's an issue you'll need to go and do your own research.

Broadly, very broadly, speaking, there are two forms available – quicker-cooking parboiled/pearled grains and slower-cooking untampered-with grains. I freely admit to opting for the former most of the time – 10 minutes or so in boiling water and they're done. The latter are more nutritious, but may need to be soaked for 12 hours or so before simmering for 25–45 minutes. Local cooks recommend leaving them to cool in their own water before draining to get the plumpest, tenderest results. In short, check and follow the packet instructions.

Insalata di Grano e Finocchio

Wheat or Farro Salad with Fennel and Carrot

Whole wheat grain salads have become one of my staples, particularly in the summer months, as part of an *antipasto* collection or for a main course with grilled fish or meat. This is the version I turn to again and again, with fennel and carrot and lots of fresh herbs and lemon juice.

Serves 6

200g dried or parboiled wheat grains or farro
1 head of fennel
1 large carrot
a good handful of mint leaves, shredded
a good handful of basil leaves, shredded
100g green olives (stone in), stoned, or 75g stoned
   weight, sliced
juice of ½–1 lemon
salt and freshly ground black pepper
3–4 tablespoons extra virgin olive oil
a big handful of rocket leaves

Cook your wheat or farro in plenty of salted boiling water according to the packet instructions and the previous notes. Drain and tip into a bowl.

Trim the fennel by first cutting a thin slice off the base and slashing off the tough stalky bits. Quarter the bulb from top to base. If you have an effective mandoline, shave the fennel quarters finely with that. Otherwise slice as thinly as you possibly can. Add to the grains. Grate the carrot coarsely and add that too.

Toss with all the remaining ingredients except the rocket, then taste and add more lemon, salt, freshly ground black pepper or oil as needed. You're after a salad with a bright fresh lemony flavour that shouts, 'I'm alive, I'm delicious, eat more of me.' Eat it right then and there, or let it sit around, covered, for a few hours for the flavours to develop and for the vegetables to soften. Either way, toss the rocket into the mix just before eating.

Grano dei Morti

Pomegranate, Chocolate, Walnut and Wheat Berry Pudding

With autumn comes the harvest and its pagan celebration, now masked in a heavy Christian cloak. Rosy-cheeked pomegranates are cracking open on the trees, figs have been dried or boiled up for fig syrup and the wheatfields are no more than stubble. The non-stop back-breaking, hot work of the summer months is drawing to a close. Time to celebrate the dead!

November 1st is an official national holiday, Ognissanti, All Saints' Day, followed by the Giorno dei Morti (All Souls' or literally day of the dead), when families head for the cemeteries to clean and spruce up their relatives' graves and to spend time with those they miss. Florists have a field day selling entire meadows of chrysanthemums.

The first year I lived here, I bowled optimistically into some of the town's *pasticcerie* (pâtisseries) to ask if they were baking anything special for either celebration. A blank, slightly puzzled 'no' all round. This recipe is something I came across by accident much later. It was traditionally cooked up in the district around Foggia, and pops up repeatedly in various forms throughout the south. For full impact, it should be eaten after midnight in the dark early hours of November 2nd, when the barriers between the worlds of the living and the dead dissolve.

You might, on the other hand, just try it out because anything with chocolate, walnuts and pomegranate seeds in it has to be worth eating at any time of the day or year. That's what I thought, anyway. It turns out I was wrong. It is a profound disappointment, dull and dutiful and a rare instance of a dish being far less than the sum of its ingredients. I include it merely as a point of interest and suggest that you absolutely don't bother trying it for yourself. It's a curiosity packed with shedloads of pagan symbolism, a relic with its echoes of magic and witchcraft, a memory of a time when treats and sweet-meats were few and far between.

cooked wheat grains
pomegranate seeds
dark chocolate, chopped
new season wet walnuts, chopped
ground cinnamon
sugar
lots of *cotto di fichi* (fig syrup)

Mix everything together some time early evening on November 1st, then sit back and wait for midnight to strike before serving with extra *cotto di fichi* for those who genuinely want to eat it, or simply leave it out for the souls of the dead to enjoy.

Orecchiette e Cavolfiore

Orecchiette with Cauliflower and Pancetta

I was tipped off to this recipe by my friend Scott, he of the divine pickled figs on page 110. Like he says, cauliflower and pasta seem an unpromising combination to someone brought up on cauliflower cheese at best, watery overcooked grey mushy cauliflower, like the miserable stuff they served at my school, at worst. Actually, my school's cauliflower cheese was pretty awful as well; it took me over a quarter of a century before I could face the combo without feeling bilious.

Italy, as you might expect, has a very different take on cauliflower. Pairing it with big, bold, umami-laden ingredients, like pancetta or anchovies, garlic and chilli, gives cauliflower an Italian swagger. No apologies, no hesitation, no blanketing it into apologetic submission. This cauliflower is the star of the pasta catwalk. A whole head for four people? But of course, because it tastes so good. Cook it with the pasta, for a full 8–10 minutes? Yes, indeedy – the perfect cauli is not al dente (that's for the pasta itself), nor mushy, just nicely cooked through and beautifully tender.

Serves 4, generously

1 small head of very fresh cauliflower, preferably the
    type with green curds
350–400g dried orecchiette or conchiglie
2 tablespoons extra virgin olive oil
1 onion, chopped
150g smoked pancetta lardons
2 cloves of garlic, chopped
1 dried red chilli, finely chopped

2 tablespoons finely chopped parsley
200g cherry tomatoes, halved
salt and freshly ground black pepper

To serve
mollica fritta (see opposite) or freshly grated pecorino
    or both

Cut and break the cauliflower into small florets, roughly 3–4cm across. Slice the stem into chunks of a similar size. Put a large pan of well-salted water on to heat up. When boiling vigorously, add the pasta. Bring back to the boil, then tip in the cauliflower and cook for another 8–10 minutes, until the pasta is almost al dente.

Meanwhile put the olive oil, onion and pancetta into a large frying pan. Fry gently until the onion is tender and translucent. Add the garlic, chilli and parsley to the pan and fry for another 30 seconds or so. Now add the tomatoes, salt and freshly ground black pepper. Let them soften and cook down into the onion mixture for a few minutes. Scoop in a ladleful of the pasta cooking water and simmer for a final 3 or 4 minutes.

By now your pasta will be cooked. Scoop out a mugful of the cooking water and reserve. Drain the pasta and cauliflower, then tip into the frying pan. Toss everything together, adding a few slurps of the reserved cooking water to keep it all moist. Serve at once, with fried breadcrumbs or pecorino cheese or both.

Mollica Fritta

Fried Breadcrumbs

Crisp fried breadcrumbs were the cheese of the poor, adding not only flavour but also crunch to the softness of pasta and vegetables. Today they still feature large in southern Italian cooking. It's amazing what you can achieve with a frying pan, a loaf of bread and some oil.

For more basic pasta dishes, keep the crumbs simple – bread and oil only – or spruce them up with garlic, chilli or fresh herbs (see page 58).

Soft breadcrumbs will take a little longer to brown than dried.

Serves 4–6

50g breadcrumbs, soft or dried or somewhere in
    between
2 tablespoons extra virgin olive oil

Put the breadcrumbs and olive oil into a frying pan and place over a medium heat. Stir to soak the breadcrumbs with the oil, then keep stirring until they turn a handsome brown. Do not be tempted to wander off for a few seconds to sort out something pressing. Stay vigilant, stay stirring. As soon as they are done, turn off the heat and scrape them out into a bowl. Use warm or at room temperature. If not using immediately, store in an airtight box in the cupboard and use within a day or two.

Fried breadcrumbs with extras

Tear up a crustless slice of bread and process with a roughly chopped clove of garlic and/or a chopped chilli and/or a small handful of roughly chopped parsley or basil, or a few sage leaves, or fresh thyme leaves. Fry as per recipe on page 57.

A Turbulent Town

There are still guides and guidebooks that tell Puglia's visitors not to bother with Taranto. Go to Bari, go to Lecce, but Taranto, over on the Ionian coast? Nah, don't bother. It's true that this is a town with a turbulent history, both ancient and modern, but precisely because of that it is salty, intriguing and real. Its emblem is an athletic youth, astride a leaping dolphin. This is Taras, son of sea god Poseidon and the nymph Satyrion, who strolled the Ionian beaches. He leans back as they ride the waves, beautiful, strong and at ease with the world.

Taranto's fate is entwined inextricably with the sea. It is a city of sailors and fishermen and heavy industry, perfectly balanced between the waters of the Ionian – the Mare Grande – on one side, and a huge, sheltered lagoon – the Mare Piccolo – on the other. For centuries it was one of the most prosperous Greek cities outside Greece until Hannibal (he of the elephants) sacked it, reducing the city to a minor entity. Still, the Romans established the mussel and oyster beds that still thrive in the lagoon, so not all bad.

In recent history, Taranto has been hit by bankruptcy and by debilitating pollution from the steel works and other factories. The handsome old town is crumbling, cats slink through its shadows, fishermen sell their wares on the harbourside. The nineteenth-century city centre bustles, while the suburbs are drab and shabby. The one thing that unites rich and poor is their conviction that the local seafood is the best. From the most basic eatery where a bowl of pasta with mussels costs just a few euros, to the glamorous city centre cafés with perfectly marshalled lines of pastries to tempt those with cash to spare, this is a place where food matters.

Riso, Fagioli e Cozze (Inverno)

Rice (or Pasta) with Cannellini Beans and Mussels (Winter Version)

This is a Taranto winter favourite, featuring, naturally, local mussels, dotted in a soupy beany cream accented with a little tomato and a swirl of best olive oil. It's true comfort food, the kind of thing that the mussel men would look forward to after a day of cold winds nipping at damp, chapped fingers out in the city's lagoon. This version is bulked out with grains of rice, but many cooks replace them with smaller pasta shapes – *ditali* (little tubes) or *macheroncini*, little macaroni elbows.

The wine is my addition – most recipes just call for water for cooking the mussels – so is not strictly necessary, but its fragrance and touch of acidity makes for an extra good bowlful.

Serves 4

250g dried cannellini beans, soaked overnight, or 500g cooked cannellini beans (tinned are fine)

1kg fresh mussels in their shells

6 sprigs of parsley

150ml white wine or water

4 tablespoons extra virgin olive oil, plus a little extra for serving

salt and freshly ground black pepper

3 cloves of garlic, finely chopped

1 red chilli, dried or fresh, finely chopped

175g passata

100g long-grain rice (or *ditalini* or other small pasta shape)

If using dried beans, drain and cook them in lightly salted boiling water until very tender. If using tinned beans, drain and rinse under the cold tap.

Meanwhile, clean the mussels (see page 70). Chop the parsley leaves and set aside. Put the stalks into a saucepan large enough to take all the mussels with room to spare, along with the wine or water. Bring up to the boil, tip in the prepared mussels and clamp the lid on firmly. Shake over a high heat for a few minutes, until the mussels have opened. Throw out any that stay stubbornly closed. Scoop the mussels out into a bowl with a slotted spoon. Let the liquid in the pan settle, then carefully pour off, leaving the sandy grit at the bottom of the pan. Save the cooking liquid, and throw out the grit and the parsley stalks. Pick the orange mussel meat out of around two-thirds of the shells.

Liquidise half the cooked beans with the cooking liquid from the mussels and 2 tablespoons of olive oil – you are aiming for a creamy, saucy consistency. Taste and add salt if needed and plenty of freshly ground black pepper. Put the whole beans and puréed beans into a saucepan, ready to heat up again. In a small frying pan, heat 2 tablespoons of olive oil. Add the garlic and chilli and fry until they begin to colour. Tip in the passata, add salt and freshly ground black pepper and simmer for another 5–10 minutes to make a thick tomato sauce.

Now, boil the rice (or pasta) in plenty of salted water until almost al dente. Drain and stir into the bean mixture. Stir in the mussels, both shucked and those still in their shell. Bring up to the boil, and simmer for a few minutes. Spoon into soup plates or bowls and spoon the tomato sauce on top. Trickle a thread of olive oil over each bowl, sprinkle with the chopped parsley leaves and serve immediately.

Pasta, Cannellini, Cozze (Estate)

Pasta with Cannellini Beans and Mussels (Summer Version)

This version of cannellini and *cozze* is lighter and fresher than the previous recipe. Pasta, beans and mussels are served in the mussel broth, with chopped fresh tomato, parsley and a touch of chilli.

Ditali means little thimbles, though in fact this pasta is more of a stubby tube about 1cm in length, hence the alternative name *tubettini*. This is the size you need for this recipe. So far, so simple. *Ditalini* are usually teensy little thimbles, the sort that go into soup, around 4mm long. *Ditaloni* are theoretically larger little thimbles, but the packet I have in my cupboard are about 1cm long, so much the same as *ditali*. Some manufacturers call all three *ditalini*, tacking on a distinctive pasta identity number (e.g. *dittalini #167*) to distinguish sizes.

Serves 4

120g dried cannellini beans, soaked overnight, or 240g cooked cannellini beans (tinned are fine)
1kg fresh mussels in their shells
6 parsley stalks
250g *ditaloni*, *ditali* or *ditalini* (see intro), or other small pasta shape
2 tablespoons extra virgin olive oil, plus a little extra for serving
2 cloves of garlic, finely chopped
1 fresh or dried red chilli, finely chopped
350g fresh tomatoes, deseeded and diced
2 tablespoons chopped parsley

a handful of basil leaves, roughly shredded
salt and freshly ground black pepper

If using dried beans, drain and cook them in lightly salted boiling water until tender. If using tinned beans, drain and rinse under the cold tap.

Meanwhile, clean the mussels (see page 70). Put the parsley stalks into a saucepan large enough to take all the mussels with room to spare, and add 250ml of water. Bring up to the boil, tip in the prepared mussels and clamp the lid on firmly. Shake over a high heat for a few minutes, until the mussels have opened. Throw out any that stay stubbornly closed. Scoop the mussels out into a bowl with a slotted spoon. Let the liquid in the pan settle, then carefully pour off, leaving the sandy grit at the bottom of the pan. Save the cooking liquid, and throw out the grit and the parsley stalks. Pick the orange mussel meat out of around two-thirds of the shells.

Shortly before serving, put a pan of lightly salted water on to boil. Add the *ditalini* and cook until almost but not quite al dente. Scoop out a mugful of the cooking water and set aside before draining the pasta.

Meanwhile, put the olive oil, garlic and chilli into a large frying pan and set over a moderate heat. Stir until the garlic just begins to change colour. Add the mussel broth, all the mussels and the beans and the mugful of pasta water and bring back to the boil. Now tip in the pasta and add the tomatoes, parsley and basil. Stir and simmer for a couple of minutes so that everything is piping hot. Drizzle with olive oil and adjust the seasoning and serve.

Spaghetti all'Assassina

Assassin's Spaghetti

This is a bawdy, bonkers, bloody brilliant pasta dish that hot-foots it from the backstreets of Bari. It breaks all the rules of pasta cooking ever written and yet, and yet . . . it vaults up there to the heavens with the very best of them. The ingredients are simple enough but it's the technique that matters: the pasta is cooked directly from dry in a heavy cast-iron frying pan, with chilli, olive oil, garlic and tomato. A degree of burn is essential to create the final brazen heap of blood-red, crisp and tender, chilli-hot, tomato-sozzled spaghetti.

Far from belonging to the grey-haired nonna's school of Italian homespun cooking, it is a relatively immature creation emanating from a professional kitchen – created back in the late 1960s in the excellent Al Sorso Preferito restaurant, which is where I still go for a plateful whenever I am in the city. There are a number of explanations for the gory name. The best, it seems to me, is the most obvious – the intense blood red of the pasta right to its core, darkened here and there with crisp, burnt threads. These days it is a Bari institution, available across the city, mostly in perfect unabashed unadorned simplicity, sometimes topped with a soothing little burrata or some other natty variation. I'm ambivalent about these and I'm not the only one; to protect the purity of the original, a group of Barese have created their own Academia dell'Assassina, which assesses and grades the offerings from restaurants throughout the city.

To try it for yourself, you will need a cast-iron frying pan which will hold the intense heat that's needed, and a degree of faith and determination. If you have any choice in the matter, choose thinner spaghetti rather than thicker, though not as thin as vermicelli. Be bold, be brazen and enjoy.

Serves 2

200g passata
4 tablespoons tomato purée
salt
3 tablespoons extra virgin olive oil
1 large clove of garlic, chopped
1 or 2 red chillies, fresh or dried, finely chopped
160–180g spaghetti

To serve
freshly grated Parmesan or pecorino
for those that need a soothing creamy counterbalance
    to the fiery taste: 2 small burrata (*burratine*)

You will also need a cast-iron frying pan large enough to comfortably take the spaghetti lying flat. Mine is actually about half a centimetre too small in diameter, so I cheat and snap the spaghetti in half. This is frowned upon in Barese kitchens, but hell, they don't need to know.

Put a quarter of the passata into a saucepan together with the tomato purée, 1 litre of water and a couple of pinches of salt. Bring to the boil, then turn the heat right down so that it remains hot but doesn't boil away. Place your frying pan over a high heat. Add the olive oil, garlic and chillies. As soon as the garlic begins to colour, pour the remaining passata into the frying pan. It will sizzle and spit, but that's as it should be. Cook for a few minutes, stirring until it has reduced by at least half, and is threatening to catch on the base of the pan.

Quickly lay the spaghetti in the pan and spread out as much as you can. Stand back for 30 seconds or so, then slide your fish slice under the spaghetti and turn it, so that the upper strands come into contact with the base of the pan. Leave to cook for a minute or two more. By now the pasta should be beginning to catch and burn. Perfect. It's up to you how dark you take it but don't forget that this is the essence of the dish.

Turn the pasta again and add 2 ladlefuls of the hot tomato broth. Let it bubble up and boil until almost all of it has evaporated, turning the spaghetti. Repeat a ladleful at a time until the pasta is just about al dente – this will take some 10–12 minutes depending on the thickness of the spaghetti. Let it frizzle for a few seconds longer, until some of the strands are crisply fried in the hot oil, while the rest stays tender. Serve straight away, spanking hot and full of exuberance. Pile on to serving plates. If you want to be fancy, perch a mini burrata on top of each one. Personally, I think this is a bit of a cop-out. Give me no more than a sprinkling of freshly grated Parmesan or pecorino and I am blissfully happy.

Cocule di Ricotta e Spinaci

Potato, Ricotta and Spinach Dumplings in Tomato Sauce (with or without horseradish)

Cocule are a lesson in how to make a little go a long way. Homely, comforting and filling, these dumplings pop up here and there in parts of Puglia, Basilicata and Calabria, in various forms depending on local custom, ingredients and taste. Aubergine, Swiss chard, courgette can all find their way into *cocule*. Ricotta is optional. The key is to make sure that the potato/bread mixture is not too damp and that it is energetically seasoned. On the rare occasions that I can lay my hands on fresh horseradish root, I grate some into the mix for a big lick of energy, but it's not an easy thing to find. Otherwise, be sure to add a large dose of freshly ground black pepper.

Serves 4

400g potatoes
120g stale bread, plus a little extra if needed
500g fresh spinach, cooked
100g ricotta, well drained
100g freshly grated pecorino or Parmesan, plus extra to finish
2 cloves of garlic, crushed
20g grated fresh horseradish root (optional)
1 egg
freshly ground black pepper

For the sauce
2 tablespoons extra virgin olive oil
2 cloves of garlic, finely chopped

1 dried red chilli, finely chopped (omit if using
    horseradish)
650ml passata
salt and freshly ground black pepper
a handful of basil, roughly shredded

Preheat the oven to 200°C/180°C fan/gas 6.

Cut the potatoes, still in their skins, into large chunks. Boil in salted water until tender. Drain and peel off the skins while still hot. Weigh out 300g of cooked potato and mash thoroughly.

Soak the bread in cold water until soft, then squeeze out all the moisture. Squeeze the spinach too, pressing to get rid of as much water as you can. Chop the spinach roughly. When it is cool, mix thoroughly with the potato, ricotta, pecorino or Parmesan, bread, crushed garlic, horseradish if using and egg. Season generously with freshly ground black pepper. No need for salt – the cheese will have salted the mix just fine. The dough needs to be firm enough to shape into balls. If it is a bit sloppy, add a little more soaked and squeezed bread. If it is too dry, add more ricotta. Divide into 12 portions and roll each one into a ball.

While the potato is cooking, make the sauce. Put the olive oil, garlic and chilli into a saucepan and fry until the garlic is just beginning to take colour. Pour in the passata, season with salt and freshly ground black pepper and stir. Simmer gently for 10 minutes. Stir in the basil.

Find a baking dish large enough to take all the potato balls in a close single layer. Spoon in a third of the sauce and spread over the base. Arrange the potato balls on top, then spoon over the remaining sauce. Dredge with more pecorino or Parmesan and bake for 20–25 minutes, until sizzling hot. Serve right away.

Impepata di Cozze

Peppery Mussels

I first came across *impepata di cozze* a gazillion years ago when I fell head over heels in love with the Amalfi coast. I was young, the sun shone, the scenery was stunning, the sea a brilliant turquoise. I took the terrifying, thrilling local bus along the high, twisting, narrow coast road from Salerno, through Vietri sul Mare, famous for its vivid ceramics and as the birthplace of the late Antonio Carluccio, through Cetara, famous for its anchovies and even better for its *colotura di alici*, the Italian equivalent of Thai fish sauce. I stopped off at Minori, Maiori, Atrani and eventually Amalfi itself (lemons, lemons, limoncello, the best ever candied peel, purportedly birthplace of the compass and home to the strangest-ever fried aubergine and chocolate custard pudding). Peppery mussels featured on every menu.

Now, here in even more southerly Italy, I find them again. A standard way to prepare mussels, like the French *moules marinières*, but even simpler. Frankly it's no more than an exaggerated pepperiness, but it makes the sweet, ozone flavour of plump mussels even sweeter and ozonier. Use freshly ground black pepper to get the full drama.

Serves 4 as a starter, 2 as a main course

1kg fresh mussels in their shells
2 cloves of garlic, chopped
2 tablespoons extra virgin olive oil
2 teaspoons freshly ground black pepper
2 tablespoons finely chopped parsley
3 or 4 big squeezes of lemon juice

Clean the mussels assiduously (see below). 10 minutes or so before you want to serve them up, put the garlic and olive oil into a saucepan large enough to hold all the mussels as well. Place over a moderate heat. As soon as the garlic begins to colour, tip in your mussels, turn the heat up high and clamp on the lid. Shake gently for around 3–5 minutes until the mussels have opened. Turn off the heat and scoop the mussels out into a bowl, discarding any that steadfastly refuse to open.

Quickly pour the juices in the pan into a bowl and let them settle for a minute or two while you rinse the pan out with water. Carefully pour the juices back into the pan, leaving behind the grit and debris at the bottom of the bowl. Return to the heat, and tip in the mussels. Add the freshly ground black pepper, parsley and a few squeezes of lemon juice. Stir and shake for a minute on a high heat, then serve steaming hot and spicy, with plenty of bread to soak up the juices.

Cleaning mussels

Ignore the tag or fishmonger that promises cleaned mussels all ready to cook. In my experience, all fresh mussels need home TLC before cooking. It's a bore, but better than a mouthful of grit or worse, a dodgy stomach. So, tip the mussels into the sink and work through them methodically, pulling away the tough beard (the byssus, which tethers them to their pole or rope or rock as they grow) and scraping off barnacles. Rinse each one well under the cold tap. Discard any that are broken, or that don't close when rapped against the work surface. Carefully pile them all back into the sink, cover with fresh cold water, swish them around gently, then leave for a couple of minutes for sand and grit to settle on the bottom. Scoop the mussels out into a colander. And repeat one more time with newly poured water to get rid of as much sand and grit as you can.

A Trio of Stuffed Aubergines

Melanzane ripiene, stuffed aubergines, are a summer staple from Puglia right through to Reggio Calabria at the tip of Calabria's toe. Inevitably every town, family and cook has their own finessed formula for absolutely and totally the best ever version that leaves all others in culinary shade. Especially the versions from neighbouring towns where they know nothing, nothing about how to stuff an aubergine in the correct manner. Always happy to join the fray, I've been working up my own versions, based on sage advice from a number of cooks including my mentors Downstairs Maria and, new addition, Fran's mum, Filomena.

Key points so far:

1. Ideally you need smaller individual-portion-sized aubergines, weighing around 150–200g each, but when you can't get those, larger aubergines will do almost as well.

2. The filling only works when you use good-quality bread. We're talking a classy *pain de campagne* or mild white sourdough or similar. It needs to be stale and dry. Cheap sliced bread makes a slimy filling.

3. Many cooks fry the aubergine shell but this is not necessary. Many cooks boil the shell for a couple of minutes to give it a head start in the oven, but stuffing the floppy boiled shell is a pain. The simplest option is simply to salt it before filling and add a slurp of water to the baking dish to help it soften in the oven.

4. *Melanzane ripiene* are either *'rosso'*, in other words bathed in tomato sauce, or *'bianco'*, without sauce. Personally, I prefer my meat-based stuffed aubergines *rosso* but the cheesy ones *bianco* so that the tops crisp up nicely. Tuna-stuffed *melanzane* are excellent either way.

Melanzane Ripiene di Carne

Stuffed Aubergines Maria-Downstairs Style

This is more-or-less how my lovely downstairs neighbour Maria makes her enormously popular stuffed aubergines.

Serves 8 as a starter, 4 as a main course

4 small aubergines (each weighing around 150–200g),
    or 2 medium aubergines
20–30g freshly grated Parmesan, pecorino or
    cacioricotta, to finish

For the stuffing
1 onion, chopped
3 cloves of garlic, chopped
3 tablespoons extra virgin olive oil, plus a little extra
    for testing
250g minced veal or beef
100g stale bread, broken into chunks
2 tablespoons finely chopped parsley
60g freshly grated Parmesan, pecorino or *cacioricotta*
2 tablespoons capers, rinsed thoroughly if salted
1 egg

For the sauce
3 cloves of garlic, chopped
1 red chilli, finely chopped
2 tablespoons extra virgin olive oil
650g passata
salt and freshly ground black pepper
a handful of fresh basil leaves, shredded

Get the sauce going first. Put the garlic, chilli and olive oil into a saucepan and set over a moderate heat. Once the garlic begins to colour, pour in the passata and 200ml of water. Season with salt and freshly ground black pepper, then simmer gently, three-quarters covered with a lid, for about half an hour. Stir occasionally to make sure it isn't catching on the base of the pan. Stir in the basil once the sauce is done.

Trim off the green stem from each aubergine, then cut them in half lengthways. Using a small knife, make criss-cross cuts in the cut surface without cutting right through. With the help of a spoon, scoop out as much of the aubergine flesh as you can, leaving an aubergine bowl about ½–1cm thick. Sprinkle the insides with salt and leave to drain, upside down, until you need them. Chop the excavated aubergine flesh roughly.

Preheat the oven to 200°C/180°C fan/gas 6. For the stuffing, put the chopped aubergine into a frying pan with the onion, garlic and 3 tablespoons of extra virgin olive oil. Fry over a moderate heat until the onion is translucent. Raise the heat and add the minced meat. Fry, breaking up the grains of meat, until it has all turned opaque. Let the mixture cool down.

Meanwhile, put the stale bread into a bowl and cover with cold water. Leave for 10 minutes to soften, then squeeze out all the water and drop the bread into a mixing bowl. Add the parsley, cheese, the cooked meat mixture, the capers, 4 tablespoons of the tomato sauce, the egg, salt and freshly ground black pepper. Mix the whole lot together really well with your hands. Fry a small knob of the mixture in a little olive oil and taste to check the seasoning. Add more salt and freshly ground black pepper if needed.

Divide the mixture into 8 (for smaller aubergines) or 4 (for larger ones) and fill each aubergine shell, mounding the mixture up generously. Arrange the filled shells in an oiled baking dish, spoon 2–3 tablespoons of water around them and then ladle the tomato sauce over the top of them, covering the filling entirely. Dredge with the grated cheese and bake for 30 minutes, until the aubergine is tender and the sauce is sizzling hot. Serve hot or warm.

Mulingiani Chjini

Very Cheesy Stuffed Aubergines, Calabrian Style

This meat-free recipe for stuffed aubergines is based on Calabrian recipes and guidance from my friend Francesco's mum, Filomena, from Basilicata. It's very cheesy and very good. This version is *'bianco'*, in other words baked naked with no tomato sauce. If you prefer the idea of a *'rosso'*, red version, use the sauce from the Melanzane Ripiene di Carne (see page 72) and bake in the same way.

Serves 8 as a starter, 4 as a main course

4 small aubergines (each weighing around 150–200g),
   or 2 medium aubergines
freshly grated Parmesan, pecorino or *cacioricotta*,
   to finish

For the stuffing
1 onion, chopped
3 cloves of garlic, chopped
4 tablespoons extra virgin olive oil, plus a little extra for
   testing
200g stale bread, broken into chunks
2 tablespoons finely chopped parsley
100g mozzarella, cut into 1cm dice
200g *caciocavallo stagionato* or *provolone*, cut into
   1cm dice
80g freshly grated Parmesan or *cacioricotta*
2 heaped tablespoons capers, rinsed thoroughly if salted
14 cherry tomatoes, roughly chopped
2 eggs
salt and freshly ground black pepper

Trim off the green stem from each aubergine, then cut them in half lengthways. Using a small knife, make criss-cross cuts in the cut surface without cutting right through. With the help of a spoon, scoop out as much of the aubergine flesh as you can, leaving an aubergine bowl about ½–1cm thick. Sprinkle the insides with salt and leave to drain, upside down, until you need them. Chop the excavated aubergine flesh roughly.

For the stuffing, put the chopped aubergine into a frying pan with the onion, garlic and 4 tablespoons of extra virgin olive oil. Fry over a moderate heat until the onion is translucent. Let the mixture cool down.

Meanwhile, put the stale bread into a bowl and cover with cold water. Leave for 10–15 minutes to soften, then squeeze out all the water and drop the bread into a mixing bowl. Add the parsley, the cheeses, the onion and aubergine mixture, the capers, tomatoes, eggs, salt and freshly ground black pepper. Mix the whole lot together really well with your hands. Fry a small knob of the mixture in a little olive oil and taste to check the seasoning – add more salt and freshly ground black pepper if needed.

Preheat the oven to 200°C/180°C fan/gas 6.

Divide the mixture into 8 (for smaller aubergines) or 4 (for larger ones) and carefully fill each aubergine shell, mounding the mixture up generously. Arrange the filled shells in a snug-fitting oiled baking dish and pour 100ml of water around them. Dredge with extra grated cheese and bake for 30 minutes, until the aubergine is tender and the filling is browned and sizzling. Serve hot or warm.

Melanzane Ripiene al Tonno

As for Mulingiani Chjini above, replacing the *caciocavallo stagionato* and mozzarella with 250g of drained, flaked tinned tuna and 5 anchovy fillets, finely chopped.

Rags to Riches, Ice Cream and Fast Food

Puglia's big break-out product, making shallow waves before Puglia was much more than a pimple on the travelling world's nose, is the burrata. It was invented in the early years of the twentieth century by a *masseria* near Andria, a natty way to use up the shreddy offcuts of mozzarella once it was shaped into taut, neat, tidy spheres. Those shreds, mixed with cream, are what you find at the heart of your burrata, spilling out seductively as you cut into it.

Puglians adore the clan of milky pale delicate cheeses that includes mozzarella and burrata. They love ricotta (made with cow's, sheep's or goat's milk or all three at once), and *giuncatta* and *primo sale* (both fresh set cheeses). For crowning pasta, pizza, sandwiches and more, they buy *stracciatella*. And *stracciatella* is . . . the shreddy off-cuts of mozzarella mixed with cream. Yes, the innards of that very same burrata.

You may recognise the word if you have a taste for Italian ice cream. Or if you have a taste for Italian soup. *Stracci* or *straccetti* means rags or shreds. *Stracciatella* ice cream contains little threads of chocolate, *stracciatella* soup contains fine threads of egg, run through a sieve into the simmering broth. Then in my butcher's shop I spy another raggedy contender, *straccetti di carne*. Thin shreds of meat – veal, lamb, pork or even chicken – tossed with a touch of olive oil and seasoned breadcrumbs are no more nor less than great fast food, Italian style.

Stracetti di Agnello

Sautéed Lamb with Crisp Breadcrumbs

Serves 4

400g lamb leg or shoulder steak
3 tablespoons extra virgin olive oil
salt and freshly ground black pepper
60g stale bread
20g freshly grated Parmesan or pecorino
1 clove of garlic, roughly chopped
a small handful of parsley leaves

To garnish
a little roughly chopped parsley
wedges of lemon

Slice the lamb thinly (½cm thick) and cut into rough pieces, the rags of the title. We're talking around 2½cm across and a little longer, but don't get too precise about it. Pile them into a bowl and drizzle over a tablespoon of olive oil. Season with a little salt and a good grind or two of black pepper. Toss the lamb with the oil so that each piece is coated.

Whizz the bread with the Parmesan or pecorino, the garlic and the parsley, to make fine breadcrumbs. Tip over the meat and mix the whole lot together so that the rags of lamb are more or less coated. You won't get a perfect coating, but get the crumbs fairly evenly distributed.

Take a wide frying pan, add the remaining oil and heat it up over a high flame. When the oil is good and hot, toss in the roughly coated meat and all its crumbs. Sauté briskly, scraping up loose crumbs, until they are golden brown. A matter of 4 or 5 minutes. By now the meat will be just cooked through. Sprinkle with parsley and serve at once, with lemon wedges to squeeze over it.

A Sweet Cuckoo in a Southern Nest

Tiramisù has made itself very much at home in Italy's south. It's far too rich to be anything but a northern interloper, of course. The roster of traditional local puddings here is short. Pastries and sticky things are for the morning, sluiced down with strong coffee. *Gelati* are for the evening *passeggiata*. For special occasions, families buy cakes and confections from the *pasticceria*. Otherwise home cooks mainly opt for *crostate* – essentially large-scale and rather dull jam tarts – and *ciambelle*, plain sponge-type cakes. No wonder restaurants have cheerily filled the gap with *tiramisù*, which ticks so many user-friendly boxes.

Some forty years ago, when *tiramisù* was beginning to make a name for itself in the UK, I decided that I didn't like it. Quite why I have avoided it for so many decades, I'll never fathom, but thankfully I've seen the light. I have finally joined the Tiramisù Fan Club and like so many new converts I am now an obsessive.

In 2021, I mourned the passing of nonagenarians Alba and Ado Campeol, within a few days of each other. *Tiramisù* was, they claimed, their child, born and nurtured, with the help of their chef, Roberto Loli Linguanotto, in their restaurant Le Beccherie in Treviso. It began with a restorative bowl of creamy *sbatudin*, a *tira me su*, literally a pull me up, made of egg yolks, sugar and cocoa, for Alba after the birth of one of her human offspring. Did she dip *savoiardi* biscuits into it as she nursed the baby? Did she while away the long, tender minutes with thoughts of the perfect pudding? Maybe. *Tiramisù* finally appeared on Le Beccherie's menu in the early 1970s, and from there it hurtled out to conquer the world.

But wait! Alba and Ado were not the only claimants to the *tiramisù* creators' crown. One hundred and sixty kilometres away, over the regional border, in Friuli Venezia Giulia, a rival emerged in the form of Norma Pielli, chef/proprietor of the Albergo Roma in Tolmezzo. For years she'd been bolstering Alpine hikers with her *fetta di mascarpone*, mascarpone slice, and she had the hand-written recipe to prove it, clearly dated 1959.

It doesn't stop there. The Accademia del Tiramisù suggests that it goes way back to the nineteenth century brothels of Treviso, whose madams whipped up *sbatudin* fortified with a shot of booze for their spent clients before they returned home to their wives. Then on to the pitch steps Carminantonio Iannaccone, born in southern Italy but by now owner of the Piedigrotta Bakery in Baltimore, named for the restaurant he ran in Treviso in the 1970s. 'I was the first chef to make a real *tiramisù*,' he insists. It was a showcase for the best local ingredients, and for his own skills in the kitchen. Nothing more, nothing less. Just a dessert. There's a rumour that an unscrupulous member of his family sold the recipe to the chef at Le Beccherie. What skulduggery!

The Accademia del Tiramisù's 'original' recipe does not include any alcohol. Most restaurants here don't slug in any booze either; they don't want to intoxicate young children, I'm told, though a measure of strong espresso seems to be totally fine for the little darlings. Personally, I think this is a mistake – a shot of liquor harmonises the richness of mascarpone, the intensity of coffee and the soft crumbling ladies' fingers. It then also means that it can be reserved for adults only, away from sticky, prying little fingers. Give them an ice lolly from the freezer and they will be happy enough.

The real issue, it seems to me, is what type of booze you stir into the coffee bath. My favourite combination so far has been a blend of sweet Strega and an intense, coffee-flavoured grappa. Marsala brings a buttery sweetness, an excellent choice, particularly when blended with a slug of brandy or rum.

If you are kinder than me and are prepared to share your *tiramisù* with non-drinkers, then by all means leave out the alcohol. It will still taste good. Take a tip from my friend Marika, doyenne of one of my favourite local cafés. Though they make a booze-free *tiramisù*, she enthusiastically drizzles a small slick of San Marzano liqueur over each slice for those who want it. Now that's a real serious treat!

Tiramisù

With its meteoric rise to world-wide fame and adulation, *tiramisù* has, inevitably, spawned innumerable variations. Even in Italy, where people are so protective of their food, there are chefs who choose to play rough with the recipe. In 2021, the winner of the creative section of the Tiramisù World Cup shockingly included prosciutto and melon. In the end, though, the original is the one that thrills and seduces, with no clever-clogs additions. It's the one I return to again and again, with relief. This is my recipe for a classic *tiramisù* with alcohol.

Serves 8

500g mascarpone
100ml espresso or very, very strong cafetière coffee
2 tablespoons Marsala, or Strega, or rum
2 tablespoons grappa, or Corretto Coffee-infused
    Grappa, or brandy
4 egg yolks
70g caster sugar
3 egg whites
2 pinches of salt
20–24 *savoiardi* biscuits or ladies' fingers/sponge
    finger biscuits
unsweetened cocoa powder

You will need a 28cm × 20cm baking tin or dish.

Get your mascarpone out of the fridge and give it plenty of time to come to room temperature. Make the coffee and let it cool. Then stir in the Marsala, Strega or rum and the grappa or brandy. Pour into a shallow dish and set aside until needed.

Whisk the egg yolks with the sugar until pale and voluptuously thick. Beginning with just a few tablespoons at a time, whisk in the mascarpone bit by bit. Wash and dry your whisk well, then whisk the egg whites with the salt in a separate bowl until they form stiff peaks. Stir a tablespoonful of the whites into the mascarpone mixture to loosen it, then fold the rest in quickly.

Smear a thin layer of the mascarpone mixture over the base of the tin or dish. One by one, dip half the biscuits into the coffee mixture, turning once, shaking off the excess, then arrange them in neat, serried ranks on the first layer of mascarpone. Spread half the remaining mascarpone mixture over them. Dust with cocoa.

Repeat these layers once more, finishing with a blanket of cocoa. Cover the top of the dish with a layer of greaseproof paper or baking parchment, then wrap in clingfilm. Slide into the fridge and resist checking on it for at least 6 hours, better still until the next day.

Either serve it from the dish, scooping out helpings with a big spoon, or cut it into neat cubes using a knife dipped into very hot water. Lift each one out carefully with a fish slice and slide as neatly as you can on to individual plates.

Condensation

Here's the strangest thing. Well, it's strange if you live in the south of Italy. Last night I cooked at a house which didn't have a single fig tree in its extensive grounds. Not one. This must have been a deliberate decision, but eradication of the ubiquitous *Ficus carica* for what reason? Does the owner have a pathological fear of figs? Or maybe wasps? I guess either is plausible. The gardens hosted acres of rosemary and olives, lavender and other characteristic plants. Just no fig trees. I know this because I searched for one to pluck a few leaves from, just as a decorative twiddle for some of the dishes I was serving. Practically anything looks prettier if it is laid on a bed of fig leaves.

Fig trees grow everywhere here (except for that garden), in town, by the roadside, at the seaside, on waste ground, on pin-neat cultivated market gardens where no weed dares poke up its head. Early varieties ripen in June, but the main crop of green and purple figs arrives in late August, so profuse and sweet and succulent. Before the deluge of fruit, though, the leaves have more to offer than mere table-setting assets. In the high afternoon heat, if you take shelter under a large fig tree you might well have inhaled a curious waft of coconut. It emanates from the foliage.

This heady scent can be harvested just like the fruit. A few leaves, used fresh on the day they are picked, are all it takes to bring an exotic aura to the table. Fig leaf oil is a revelation on tomatoes or drizzled over steamed green beans. Add mint leaves, toasted sesame seeds, salt and freshly ground black pepper and you could almost be in Bali. Infuse them in cream and you have the basis for scented baked custards or pannacotta.

When my friend Sammy Jo Squire came out to help us filming here in Puglia, she somehow found the time to knock up the most voluptuous, decadent fig leaf ice cream. She happens to be one of the leading British TV home economists – you're bound to have seen her food on any number of television series and films – so no surprise that she co-ordinated crew lunches, dishes-that-I-made-earlier and soul-restoring treats in a strange kitchen miles from anywhere.

The magic ingredient, other than the fig leaves, was a tin of condensed milk. And that reminded me of the ultra-simple no-churn lemon ice cream I used to make years ago. So here we go, two doddlingly easy recipes for cooling summer desserts. No ice cream maker needed, soft-scooping straight from the freezer and utterly delicious.

Gelato di Foglie di Fichi di Sammy

Sammy's Fig Leaf Ice Cream

This is Sammy's take on fig leaf ice cream. I like to toast the fig leaves lightly before simmering them in the cream (it deepens the flavour), but if you are in a hurry, skip this stage. The salt is a masterstroke, so don't leave it out. Serve the ice cream with summer fruit or instead of vanilla ice cream with pies or tarts. Sit back and bask in the compliments.

Serves 8

5–6 fig leaves, depending on size, rinsed clean and dried
600ml double cream
1 x 397ml tin of condensed milk
1 teaspoon vanilla extract or paste
1 teaspoon crumbled flaky salt

Put a heavy-based frying pan or griddle over a high heat. When it is hot, lay a couple of fig leaves in it. Toast them for a few seconds on each side, turning them frequently until the edges curl inwards. Repeat with the remaining leaves. Put them into a saucepan with the cream. Simmer gently for 10 minutes, then leave to cool. Strain and squeeze the fig leaves to extract the last of the cream from them.

Whisk the cream into the condensed milk along with the vanilla and salt. Pour into a shallow freezer container, cover and freeze for at least 5 hours or until set solid.

Gelato di Limone

Super-Speedy Lemon Ice Cream

Serves 5–6

5–6 large lemons
1 x 397ml tin of condensed milk

Finely grate the zest from 2 of the lemons. Halve 5 of the lemons and squeeze the juice out. Gradually beat the juice into the condensed milk. Taste – it should be a bit on the sharp side, just enough to make you pause. Freezing will dampen the flavour a little. If it seems too sweet, add some or all of the juice from the final lemon. Stir in the lemon zest. Pour into a freezer container, cover and freeze for at least 5 hours or until set hard.

Olio di Foglie di Fico

Fig Leaf Oil

A bit of fun to add a lightly glamorous waft of coconut and green leaf scent to a simple salad or grilled fish. I've tried making it with olive oil but it was a mistake. The intensity of the olive masked the fragrance of the leaves. Far better to use a neutral oil as the base. Fig leaf oil has a short shelf-life, so there's little point in making litres of it unless you plan to feed an army.

Makes 130–140ml

3–4 newly picked fig leaves, depending on size
150ml sunflower oil

Put a heavy-based frying pan or griddle over a high heat. When it is hot, lay a couple of fig leaves in it. Toast them for a few seconds on each side, turning them frequently until the edges curl inwards. Repeat with the remaining leaf/leaves. Rip them up roughly and drop them into a liquidiser jug. Add the oil and blitz for a few seconds to blend. Set aside for half an hour to allow the oil to soak up the fig leaf scent. Drain through a sieve lined with muslin or a coffee filter, pressing down to extract as much oil as you can. Discard the debris. Store the oil, covered, in the fridge for up to a week.

Zeppole di San Giuseppe, Fritte o al Forno

Choux Buns, Fried or Baked, with Cherries

Fathers' day in Italy is celebrated on March 19th, the Festa di San Giuseppe, aka Jesus's earthly father, Saint Joseph. *Zeppole* are the go-to pastry: puffy swirls of dough, rich and indulgent, with a glossy cherry perched on top. The name is not, I'm disappointed to say, anything to do with air-borne zeppelins, which are named after their inventor, Count Ferdinand von Zeppelin.

In most *pasticcerie*, enthusiastic patrons can choose between the fried variety or the plainer baked version. Both are made with choux pastry, both filled with *crema pasticcera*, but inevitably *zeppole fritte* are the best. Of course they are, damn it. Still, the baked ones don't exactly consitute diet food either. How could a filled choux puff be anything short of delicious?

The essential finishing touch is an Amarena cherry, a sour cherry preserved in a heavy sugar syrup which brings a shot of glamour to the whole bundle. When I make *zeppole* I bury a second one in the centre. This is not at all how it is meant to be done, but the burst of sweet sharp fruitiness is so fabulous against the rich paleness of the *crema* that I can't resist. You should be able to pick up a jar of Amarena cherries in a classy supermarket or an Italian deli. With their trace of sharpness, they have far more character than glacé cherries, which are not a good substitute, and don't even think about using a maraschino cherry.

If you are going all out for fried *zeppole* they still need to be baked first so that they hold their shape, and remember that they have to be eaten on the day they are made. Twenty-four hours later they'll be greasy and flabby. Simpler baked choux puffs need just a tad longer in the oven, and can be stored, unfilled, in an airtight container for up to 24 hours. Warm them through for 5 minutes in the oven to restore their crispness, or deep-fry them!

Makes 6–8

For the choux pastry
125ml water
50g butter, cut into small cubes
65g plain flour
5g caster sugar
a pinch of salt
2 eggs, beaten
sunflower oil, for frying (optional)

For the *crema pasticcera*
175ml milk
2 egg yolks
35g caster sugar
½ teaspoon vanilla extract
20g plain flour

To finish
12–16 Amarena cherries, or other cherries in syrup
icing sugar

Begin with the *crema pasticcera*. Heat the milk until it is steaming and very nearly boiling. Meanwhile, whisk the egg yolks with the sugar and vanilla extract, then whisk in the flour. Pour in the hot milk, whisking constantly. Rinse out the pan. Return the custard mixture to the clean pan and place over a medium heat. Bring up to the boil, whisking constantly, scraping the thickening *crema* from the base and sides of the pan. Once the mixture is hot enough to burp big bubbles, cook for a minute more, still whisking. Draw off the heat and scrape out into a bowl. Smooth it down, then cover the surface with clingfilm and leave to cool. Just before using, warm slightly to soften it, then scoop into a piping bag fitted with a 1½cm star nozzle.

Preheat the oven to 190°C/170°C fan/gas 5. Make a template for piping out the *zeppole* – draw 6cm circles on two sheets of baking parchment, leaving at least 4cm between them. Turn them over so that the ink is underneath, and lay them on two baking trays.

Now the choux pastry. Put the water and the butter into a saucepan and place over a low heat. Let it warm gently, making sure that the butter has completely melted before the water starts to boil. While it heats, mix the flour with the sugar and salt and have them standing by ready to go. As soon as the water/butter mixture comes to the boil, take off the heat and quickly tip in the flour in one fell swoop. Beat it in, then return it to a low heat, beating the mixture until it forms a ball and leaves a very thin white film over the base of the pan. Transfer to a mixing bowl. Spread it a little way up the sides, then leave for 5 minutes or so until tepid.

Beat the eggs, a slurp at a time, into the dough until just a tablespoonful is left. You may not need it all. The final mixture should be thick and glossy. Scoop out a spoonful and inspect the peak left behind in the bowl – it needs to be stiff, but just flopping over at the top. The dough on the spoon should drop off the spoon easily without any help. If it fails the tests, whisk in a little of the remaining egg. Check again and add more as needed. Transfer the dough to a piping bag fitted with an 18mm star nozzle. Use it while still warm.

Starting in the centre of each circle and spiralling out, pipe a base of choux pastry. Spiral a second layer on top, heading into the centre, slightly smaller than the first. Dampen your finger and smooth down the peak. Slide into the oven and bake for 25–30 minutes, until puffed and nicely browned. Do not open the door for at least the first 20 minutes.

Baked zeppole Quickly pierce the top of each bun with a skewer and return to the oven for a final 5 minutes. Turn the oven off, prop the door slightly ajar and leave in the oven for another 20 minutes or so. Cool on a wire rack.

Fried zeppole Bake for just 20 minutes and when nearly done, heat a 6cm depth of sunflower oil to 170°C. Deep-fry the buns, just a few at a time, for around 3 minutes, turning once or twice. Drain on a tray or plate lined with a double layer of kitchen paper.

To finish your *zeppole*, make a hole in the top of each one with a small knife and swing it around inside to make space for the filling. Pop in a cherry, then fill up with *crema pasticcera*. Finish with a neat swirl on top. Dust with icing sugar, pop a cherry on top and they are ready to go.

Bignè di San Giuseppe

St Joseph's Fritters

These are a simpler, homelier version of the *zeppole*. No faffing around with frying <u>and</u> baking – here we cut straight to the deep-fryer. The ingredients are much the same minus the cherries, so I like to add a bit of lemony lift to the *crema pasticcera*. These *bignè* really need to be eaten warm, as soon as they are filled and rolled in sugar.

Makes around 20–25

1 quantity of *crema pasticcera* (page 91)
finely grated zest of 1 lemon
2 tablespoons limoncello
1 quantity of choux pastry (page 91)
sunflower oil, for deep-frying
caster sugar

Make the *crema pasticcera*, stirring in the lemon zest and limoncello as soon as it is cooked. Warm it gently shortly before using and spoon into a piping bag (no need for a nozzle).

Make the choux pastry as on page 92. Heat up a 6cm depth of sunflower oil to 170°C. Carefully drop dessertspoonfuls of the choux mixture into the hot oil and fry, turning occasionally, until browned all over and well puffed. As they puff, the outside layer will split here and there – keep on frying them, turning so that the pale exposed dough browns too. Drain on a tray or plate lined with a double layer of kitchen paper.

As soon as they have cooled enough to handle, make a hole in each one, and pipe in plenty of the filling. Roll in caster sugar and serve at once.

A Celebration of Multiplicity

Puglia's favourite nibble is undoubtedly the *tarallo*, a crisp little ring of savoury dough that comes in two fundamental forms – boiled and baked like a bagel, or plain baked. I champion the plain baked variety but am not averse to the glossy boiled version either. In the early months of my life here, I was determined to try my hand at making them. The results were nicely edible but honestly? All that time twiddling short strips of dough around my finger – it just wasn't worth the bother when I could buy them around the corner at Mimmo's deli for little more than they cost to make. What I did get out of the whole experience was the formula for a classic dough that has a multitude of alternative, way more satisfying uses.

Besides *taralli*, this wine-and-olive-oil-slaked dough is the base for a host of sweets, conjured up for celebrations throughout the year. At Christmas it is transformed into sticky mounds of *purciduzzi*, spangled with coloured sugar strands, or into wheels of spiralling deep-fried *cartellate*. December 13th is Saint Lucy's day, sweetened by *occhi di Santa Lucia*, iced *taralli*.

An enriched form of the dough, with eggs, is now my go-to pastry recipe for any number of pies, but is also essential for making *chiacchiere di carnevale*, crisp strips dusted with icing sugar for the run-up to Lent.

Plain Taralli Dough

140g 00 flour or plain flour
a pinch of salt
40g dry white wine
40g extra virgin olive oil

Tip the flour into a mixing bowl, add a pinch of salt and make a well in the centre. Warm the wine and oil together until hot but not boiling. Pour into the flour well and mix to form a soft dough. Knead for about 5 minutes, until silky smooth. Form into a ball, wrap in clingfilm or a beeswax wrap, and leave on one side to rest for about half an hour.

Rich Taralli Dough

400g plain flour
2 good pinches of salt
1 egg
100g dry white wine
100g extra virgin olive oil

Tip the flour into a bowl and add the salt. Make a well in the centre. Break the egg into the well and add the wine and olive oil. Use your fingers to mix the oil, egg and wine in the well, gradually drawing in the flour to form a smooth glossy dough. Knead for a few minutes, until smooth. Form into a ball, wrap in clingfilm or a beeswax wrap, and leave to rest at room temperature, or in the fridge in hot weather, for half an hour before using.

Purciduzzi

Honey-Soaked Christmas Pastry Nuggets

In the few years that I've lived here in Ceglie Messapica, the Corso Garibaldi, our rather short pedestrianised main street, has noticeably up-scaled despite or perhaps because of the fallow Covid years. Even so, the star remains the Café Centrale with its handsome façade and equally handsome pastries inside. It was here that I was introduced to Puglia's sweetest Christmas treat, the delightfully named *purciduzzi*. The little nuggets of dough are, supposedly, reminiscent of *piccoli porcinelli*, tiny piglets, transformed in dialect to *purciduzzi*. Further along the coast, into Calabria, they become *turdilli*, and head up coast from there to Naples and we have *struffoli*. All pretty much the same thing.

Whatever they are called, they are easy to make, no more than knoblets of *taralli* dough deep-fried and drenched in honey or our sweet, dark fig syrup. Fried whole almonds are a Ceglie addition and a brilliant one at that. Don't leave them out.

Stored in an airtight container, *purciduzzi* will keep for a week or more.

Serves 8–10

1 portion of plain *taralli* dough (page 97)

To finish
sunflower oil, for frying
50g whole blanched almonds
150g honey or *cotto di fichi* (fig syrup)
hundreds and thousands/coloured sugar strands

Unwrap the dough and divide into 6 pieces. Roll each one out to make a long thin sausage roughly 1cm in diameter. With a sharp knife or a dough cutter, cut into 1cm lengths.

Pour a 2cm or so depth of oil into a medium saucepan and heat to 170°C. Line a tray or a large plate with a double layer of kitchen paper. When the oil is hot, carefully slide in the almonds and deep-fry until golden brown. Scoop out with a slotted spoon and leave to drain on the kitchen paper. Now add about half the little nuggets of dough to the oil and deep-fry for 4–5 minutes, until a light biscuit brown. Scoop out on to the plate with the almonds. Repeat with the remaining dough.

Heat the honey in a small saucepan until almost boiling. Take off the heat and immediately tip in the fried dough nuggets and almonds. Stir delicately to coat in honey without breaking up the pieces. Scrape out in a heap on to a serving plate, scatter with hundreds and thousands and eat warm or cold.

Cartellate

Honey Drizzled Christmas Spirals

Cartellate are fiddly to make and a degree of patience is required. I describe the method here, but unless you are familiar with them, it probably won't make any sense. If you want to give them a go, your best bet is to search *'cartellate pugliesi'* on YouTube and watch the shaping process carefully.

When you are rolling out the dough, folding and rerolling once or twice gives a straighter edge to the final strip of pastry, as well as strengthening the dough and trapping tiny pockets of air which will bubble up crisply as the pastry is fried. Note that it is essential to let the shaped pastries dry for at least 5 hours and longer if possible before frying, otherwise they will distort in the hot oil.

Makes 6

1 portion of plain *taralli* dough (page 97)
a little plain flour

To finish
sunflower oil, for frying
150g honey or *cotto di fichi* (fig syrup)

Put a little water into a bowl ready to moisten the dough when you need it. Divide the dough in half. Wrap one half back up to keep it from drying out. Roll the other half out on a lightly floured board to form a rectangle. Fold into three, then roll out again into a long narrow rectangle. Cut lengthways into 3cm wide strips with a pastry wheel if you have one, a sharp knife if not.

Take the first strip and fold it loosely in half lengthways. Lightly dampen one end and pinch together. Dab a little water on one side of the dough 2cm further on and bring the sides together, pinching firmly. Repeat all the way along the strip. The aim is to end up with a length of little cups (which will eventually capture drops of honey) all joined together. Now curl up loosely, pinching the cups together as you go, to form a round spiral pastry. Repeat with the rest of the dough. Leave them all to dry, upside down, on a lightly floured board for at least 5 hours, or better still overnight, until firm.

Pour a 3cm or so depth of oil into a medium saucepan and heat to 170°C. Deep-fry the *cartellate* 2 or 3 at a time until golden brown and cooked through. Drain on a plate lined with a double layer of kitchen paper. Warm the honey or *cotto di fichi* until runny and drizzle generously over the *cartellate*. Eat straight away or store in an airtight container for up to a week.

Occhi di Santa Lucia

Saint Lucia's Eyes

Poor Santa Lucia had a rough time. She was born into a noble family in Syracusa in Sicily but they fell on hard times when her father died. Naturally, she was exceptionally beautiful, with luminous, pale eyes that bewitched all who saw her. She was also very devout. She rejected the advances of a noble but pagan suitor, who proceeded to denounce her to the heathen authorities. At some point (narratives vary) either he or those brutal authorities had her seductive eyes gouged out and then she was put to death. RIP Santa Lucia.

But those eyes, those beautiful, beguiling eyes . . . Italians just couldn't forget them. To this day the *occhi di Santa Lucia* are memorialised in two diverse forms: these little round, iced biscuits and the opercula of the large sea snail, *Bolma rugosa*. The operculum is the trapdoor that the snail protects itself with when it retreats into its shell. This particular one is a rather lovely, hard white spiral that you may find on beaches if you are lucky. Not edible but often used in jewellery.

Makes around 30

1 heaped teaspoon aniseed or fennel seeds
1 quantity of basic *taralli* dough (page 97)

For the icing
250g icing sugar, sifted
40ml very hot water
¼ teaspoon vanilla extract

Preheat the oven to 170°C/150°C fan/gas 3. Line a baking tray with baking parchment. Knead the aniseed or fennel seeds into the dough. Take a knob of dough (wrap the rest up in clingfilm so that it doesn't dry out) and roll out to form a long thin pencil shape. Cut into 10cm lengths. One at a time, roll around your finger, dab one end with a little water and seal to form a ring. Lay on the lined baking tray and repeat with the rest of the dough. Bake for 20–25 minutes until a pale biscuit colour.

Meanwhile, make the icing: mix the icing sugar with the hot water and vanilla. One by one, dip the baked dough into the icing. Leave on a wire rack to dry. *Finito*. Best served and eaten fairly swiftly.

Chiacchiere di Carnevale

Chattering Carnival Pastries

The run-up to Lent is carnival season, spanning the darkest, coldest months of the year. As I write this on a February afternoon, there are flurries of snow outside. Yes, snow in Puglia is a regular occurrence, though it rarely settles. Head up into the hills of Basilicata and Calabria and it's a different story. Winter white-outs and heavy frosts are common enough. Treats and parties and traditional rituals mark off the days before spring brings an easier life. *Chiacchiere* are everywhere – in *pasticcerie*, supermarkets and kitchens. Rustling, crisp, rich and sugary, and so good when still warm from the pan, though they keep well in an airtight container if you can't eat them all at once. *Chiacchiere* literally translates as to chat or chatter, and that's exactly what you should do – share them with friends and family, chatting together as your teeth shatter the crisp dough.

Makes enough for a small crowd

1 quantity of rich *taralli* dough (page 98)
a little plain flour
sunflower oil, for frying
icing sugar

Line a tray with a clean tea towel and dust with flour. Divide the dough into 4 portions. Keep three of them wrapped in clingfilm or a beeswax wrap to prevent them drying out. Roll the dough out on a lightly floured work surface to form a rough rectangle. Fold in three to give you straight edges, then roll out again. This time get it as thin as you can – you're aiming for no more than a couple of millimetres. Using a pastry wheel or a sharp knife, cut into 15cm × 6cm rectangles. Make a cut down the centre of each one (just partway) but don't cut in half. Lay them on the floured tea towel without overlapping. Repeat with the remaining dough.

Line a second tray with a double layer of kitchen paper. Pour a 3–4cm depth of oil in a saucepan and heat to 170°C. Deep-fry the *chiacchiere* 3 or 4 at a time (more if it is a larger pan, but don't overcrowd the oil), until a light biscuit colour. Drain on kitchen paper while you fry the rest. Dust generously with icing sugar and eat warm or store in an airtight box once completely cool. They'll keep for a week or so.

Cotognata Spalmabile

Quince, Honey and Lemon Jam

Spall-maaa-beee-lay, *spall-maaa-beee-lay*, SPALL-MAAA-BEEE-LAY! I so love the way this word rolls through and round the mouth as I say it. It just means 'spreadable', which is an honest, functional word but one which brings scant vocal joy. *Cotognata spalmabile* is a recipe for a totally joyful spreadable quince paste.

It is, naturally, a beautiful thing to spread over buttery toast on a chilly winter morning, but don't leave it at that. Here in the south of Italy, smooth sweet jams like this are often served with cheeses – fab with a matured *caciocavallo* and equally good with a handsome slice of farmhouse Cheddar or Wensleydale. It goes very nicely with roast lamb, or with duck. Stir a spoonful or two into the Christmas gravy, or spread a thin layer over the pastry base of an apple or custard tart before filling and baking.

Last time I made this I began with approximately 2kg of quinces but they were windfalls from trees that had never been chemically cajoled into producing perfect fruit. They arrived with bruises and blemishes here and there. After peeling and coring and removing the damaged sections, I ended up with just over a kilogram of prepared fruit, which yielded 5 medium jars of the finished *cotognata*. With perfect fruit, you may end up with a jar or two more.

quinces

Per kg of quince purée
150g honey
600g caster sugar or granulated sugar

finely grated zest and juice of 1 large lemon, or 1½
    smaller lemons

Peel and core the quinces and cut out any bruised or discoloured parts. Cut what's left into chunks and pile into a large saucepan. Add enough water to cover – I reckon you need around 1.25 litres of water per kilo of prepared fruit, but exact quantities will depend on the depth and width of the saucepan. Simmer for 40–60 minutes, until the quince is very soft. Meanwhile, wash and sterilise your jam jars (see below).

Let the mixture cool slightly, then either rub through a sieve or put through a mouli-légumes, or whizz to a purée in a food processor. Weigh the resulting purée, then scrape into a large saucepan. For each kilogram of purée, add 150g of honey, 600g of sugar and the finely grated zest and juice of 1 large lemon. Stir the mixture together over a moderate heat. Cook, stirring frequently to prevent catching, until the mixture is very thick. The line left when you drag a spoon through it should stay clearly visible for a good 10 seconds or more. Timing-wise we're looking at around 15–20 minutes, but it could be longer if you began with a runnier purée.

Ladle into the hot sterilised jam jars. If you have waxed jam discs, cover the surface of the jam with these, smoothing down gently to expel trapped air. If not, seal the jars and quickly turn them upside down. Leave to cool. Label, then store in a cool, dark cupboard until you are ready to dig in. Once opened, store in the fridge.

Sterilising jam jars

Preheat the oven to 170°C/150°C fan/gas 3. Wash the jam jars and lids in warm soapy water. Rinse, then place the jars upside down on a rack in the oven for around 15 minutes to dry and heat through. If the lids are pure metal, put them into the oven too. More likely they will have a plastic lining, in which case simmer for 10 minutes in boiling water before using. Fill and seal the jars while they are still hot.

Scott's Pickled Figs

It is late August and the figs are ripe. They are everywhere, bursting open to reveal the tender, pink, seedy heart. The small green figs are the sweetest and most abundant, but swollen purple figs are arguably (and we do argue it) more flavourful. I stop at the roadside to gather them in from unharvested trees. Locals dry them, halved and oozing nectar, on cane drying racks, or boil them up for jam or syrup. Friends thrust bags of figs towards me. Best of all, however, is the gift of a jar of pickled figs from my friend Scott. The halved figs are neatly displayed cut side to glass, pretty as a picture, dotted with whole pink peppercorns from the tree in his garden. They are totally gorgeous, wonderful with *prosciutto crudo* or burrata. I use them in salads with watermelon, rocket and mozzarella. Seared in a fearsomely hot pan for a few seconds, they are just fab with good meaty pork sausages, or alongside a quick rare-roast duck breast.

I've plundered the recipe, with Scott's permission, from his detailed Eat Puglia pages on his Gay Puglia Podcast website (gaypugliapodcast.com).

For 1 large jar

500ml white wine vinegar
300g caster sugar
1 teaspoon fennel seeds
8 black peppercorns
8 pink peppercorns
3 bay leaves
400g just-ripe figs
3 sprigs of thyme

First make the pickling liquid. Put all the ingredients except the figs and thyme into a non-reactive saucepan. Bring gently up to the boil, stirring occasionally to dissolve the sugar. Simmer for 2 minutes, then leave to cool. Scoop out and reserve the spices and bay leaves.

Halve the figs, cutting from stem to base. Arrange them loosely in a sterilised preserving jar, interspersing with fennel seeds, peppercorns, bay leaves and thyme. Heat the pickling liquid back up, then pour over the figs, making sure that they are completely submerged. Seal tightly, label and store in a cool, dark cupboard for at least 3 days before using. Unsealed, they keep well for 2–3 months. Once opened, store in the fridge for up to a week.

Zucca sott'olio

Griddled Winter Squash Pickles

In these lands where olive trees have spread their silvery branches over parched summer earth for centuries, it is inevitable that the limpid green-gold oil plays its part in preserving foods for the colder winter months. Even autumn's hard-skinned *zucca*, orange-fleshed squashes, don't keep for ever, and this is one of my favourite ways to preserve them for a month or two longer than Mother Nature. The trick is to griddle (or chargrill) them over a belting heat until two-thirds softened with a just a touch of firmness in the centre, to give a smoky sweet-sour pickle to eat with cheeses or cured meats into the spring and early summer.

Makes 2–3 jars

1kg butternut squash or other firm-fleshed winter
   squash
around 500ml extra virgin olive oil
400ml white wine vinegar
40g salt
50g caster sugar
6 cloves of garlic, halved
6 small dried red chillies
either: 2 sprigs of rosemary, snapped in half
or: 3 star anise, 2 cinnamon sticks

Trim the seeds and peel from the squash, then slice as thinly as you can. We're talking about 5mm, give or take. Put into a bowl and add 2 tablespoons of extra virgin olive oil. Mix so that all the pieces of squash are lightly coated with oil. Put your griddle pan (or a heavy-based wide frying pan) over a high heat and leave for 4–5 minutes, until scarily hot. Arrange the pieces of squash, without overlapping, on the griddle pan and leave for a couple of minutes until striped with brown. Turn over and repeat on the other side. Unless you have a massive griddle, you'll have to do this in batches.

Meanwhile, stir the vinegar, salt and caster sugar together in a mixing bowl. Drop the griddled squash into this mixture as soon as it is done. Mix carefully, then leave to marinate for 3–4 hours. Drain well. Spread a couple of clean tea towels on a tray (or two), spread the squash out on the tea towels, then cover with a couple more tea towels. Pat down, then leave to dry for another couple of hours or overnight.

Sterilise your preserving jars (see page 108), upturn on a wire rack and leave to dry and cool. Turn them right way up and pour a thin layer of oil over the base. Add a couple of layers of squash. Next add a couple of bits of garlic, a chilli and a 4cm sprig of rosemary, or a short length of cinnamon stick and a few petals of star anise. Pour in more olive oil to cover. Repeat the layers until the jar is almost full, finishing with a layer of squash. If using star anise and cinnamon, include just one star anise and a 5cm length of cinnamon in each jar. You want to leave roughly 1cm unfilled. Press down gently, then cover completely with olive oil. Screw the lids on loosely, then set aside for a couple of hours to settle. Top up with oil if necessary. The squash needs to be totally covered in oil. Seal tightly, label, then tuck away at the back of a cupboard for at least 2 weeks before using.

The pickles are at their best eaten within 3 months. Remember to store the jars in the fridge once opened, where they will keep for up to 2 weeks.

Lo Cherry

Cherry and Red Wine Liqueur

Lino's restaurant has been a haven for me over the years I've lived here. In the winter, the small interior is warm and welcoming with its idiosyncratic collection of artwork; in the summer, tables spill out on to the sloping road outside, packed every night with revellers who have no qualms about eating at an angle. The *antipasto* is the best in town and at the other end of the meal comes the crowning glory – *lo cherry*. It took me a while to realise that what was being offered was not a shot of sherry but Lino's own cherry and red wine liqueur.

Makes about 1½ litres

500g ripe cherries
a handful of cherry leaves (optional)
500ml 96% proof alcohol or 600ml vodka
350g caster sugar
250ml Primitivo wine

Stone the cherries over a bowl to catch the juice. Save 8 of the cherry stones and crack them open with a hammer. Put the cherry leaves, if using, the cherries, their juice and the cracked stones into a wide-mouthed preserving jar. Pour in the alcohol/vodka. Seal tightly and leave on the side for 2 weeks, shaking the jar occasionally.

Put the sugar into a saucepan. If you've used 96% proof alcohol, add 250ml water. If using vodka, make that a mere 170ml. Stir over a moderate heat, until the sugar has completely dissolved. Leave to cool.

Strain the cherry liquid from the jar into a large bowl. Stir in the Primitivo and the sugar syrup. Decant the mixture into bottles, seal tightly, label, then leave in the cupboard for another 2 weeks at least before sampling.

Don't bin the boozy cherries

Once the cherry liquid has been strained off, the cherries themselves remain. Admittedly, much of their flavour has disappeared into the alcohol, but it would be a crying shame to bin them. Pick out and discard the leaves and cracked stones, then tip the cherries into a sterilised preserving jar. Make up another batch of sugar syrup – 250ml of water to 350g of caster sugar – and pour it over them. Seal tightly and set aside for a week or two (they'll keep for several months). I like them spooned over ice cream or folded into ricotta with a little vanilla, chopped dark chocolate and toasted almonds. They are excellent baked into cakes too, a grown-up alternative to the glacé cherry.

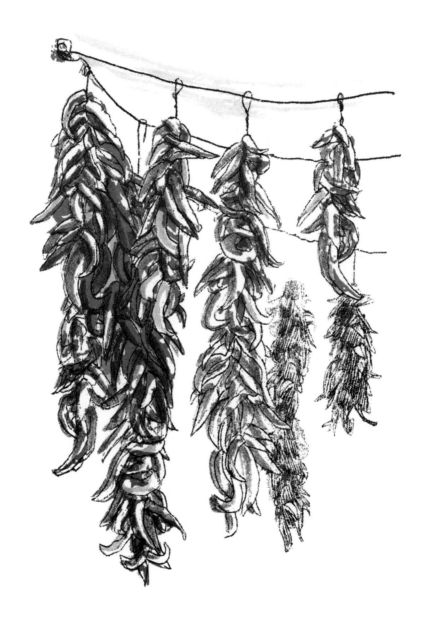

Basilicata

From the Sassi to Agliano, a Pilgrimage of Sorts

Lucania '61 is an extraordinary painting on many levels. It's long, nearly two metres of it. It stretches the length of the room, telling story after story of life in Basilicata in the first half of the twentieth century. The faces are lined and serious, worn with the constant struggle of raising large families in crowded one-room homes, shared with animals, working long, heavy hours, little money, no sanitation.

It was painted by Carlo Levi, better known as the author of *Christ Stopped at Eboli*, a book that has left a lasting imprint in my mind ever since I first read it many years ago. I was rereading it as I began a small pilgrimage of sorts in Matera last year. The painting is on display here in the Museo Nazionale d'Arte Medievale e Moderna, in the halls of Palazzo Lanfranchi in the smart boulevards at the top of the ravine.

Just a few metres away you enter a different world. The land drops away into the vast maze of narrow streets and stairways that make up the Sasso Caveoso and the Sasso Barisano. This labyrinth of cave houses was once one of Italy's most notorious slums. In 1935, Carlo Levi's sister Luisa, a neuropsychiatrist, was horrified when she visited: '. . . I could see into the caves, whose only light came in through the front doors. Some of them had no entrance but a trapdoor and ladder. In these dark holes with walls cut out of the earth I saw a few pieces of miserable furniture, beds and some ragged clothes hanging up to dry. On the floor lay dogs, sheep, goats, and pigs. Most families have just one cave to live in and there they sleep all together; men, women, children and animals. This is how twenty thousand people live.'

The inhabitants of the Sassi were nearly all rehomed in the 1950s in a mass slum clearance project. These days the slums are transformed with boutique hotels, restaurants and shops and hordes of tourists.

Luisa Levi was on a slow, torturous journey to visit Carlo, who had been exiled by Mussolini from the north of Italy to Aliano, a godforsaken village in the back of beyond, in the heart of nowheres-land Basilicata. This was where I was heading next.

Nowadays it's an easy drive, even in the rain. The village is full of memories of the man who immortalised it in words and paint. His house, now a museum, was, inevitably, closed for the winter, but discreet plaques lead the Levi pilgrim through the streets, and the memories of the peasants who drew him into their lives.

The Contadina Sisina restaurant is a modest affair, but it turned out to be the highlight of my journey. After a joyous array of *antipasti* and a bowl of pasta, I met Sisina herself. We talked of cooking and the dishes I'd eaten, then of Carlo Levi. 'Oh yes,' she smiled, 'my father was Giovannino, the boy with the goat.' I'd seen his portrait that very morning in Matera. She showed me photos of Carlo Levi with the ragtaggle gaggle of scruffy little boys that followed him through the village and watched him paint among the olive trees and cypresses at the top of the village. I wiped a tear away, hugged Sisina and her family and retired to bed.

Contadina Sisina's Involtini di Melanzane al Latte di Capra

Aubergine Rolls Baked in Goat's Milk

Among the many local dishes included in Contadina Sisina's *antipasto*, this one stood out a mile. First, because it was creamy and that in itself is unusual in this part of the world. Second, because I couldn't quite identify the key flavour. The heat of the oven brings a hint of caramel to the milk, but there was something more in there. Later Sisina revealed her secret – milk from the herd of goats that graze in the rough land around the village.

Serves 4 as a first course

1 large aubergine
a little extra virgin olive oil
30g breadcrumbs
1 tablespoon chopped parsley
1 tablespoon capers, rinsed thoroughly if salted
20g freshly grated Parmesan
salt and freshly ground black pepper
1 egg, beaten
50g thinly sliced mortadella
200ml goat's milk

Preheat the oven to 220°C/200°C fan/gas 7. Slice the aubergine thinly lengthways. Brush the slices with olive oil, lay them on a baking tray and roast for about 10 minutes. Check them and take out any that are already tender and floppy. Turn the rest over and return to the oven for another 5–10 minutes, until they are all just cooked through. Leave to cool.

To make the filling, mix the breadcrumbs with the parsley, capers, Parmesan, salt and freshly ground black pepper, and just enough egg to bind. Cut the mortadella into the same number of pieces as you have slices of aubergine.

Spread the aubergine slices out in front of you, season with salt and freshly ground black pepper and lay a piece of mortadella on each one, towards the wider end. Divide the breadcrumb mixture between them. Fold the sides over, then roll them up as neatly as you can. Arrange them in a single layer in a small, close-fitting baking dish. They can be prepared to this point 2–3 hours in advance. Keep them covered and store some- where cool.

Pour the goat's milk over them and bake for 20–25 minutes, until bubbling, browning and hot, hot, hot. Serve as soon as they can be eaten without burning your mouth.

Cialledda Calda

Matera's Winter Vegetable Casserole

This is a dish that has become something of a favourite of mine. It's simple, comforting and nurturing, with a healthy dose of vegetables. The recipe has emerged from the fireplace kitchens of the Sassi in the smoky cave houses of the poor, but remains a meal that the inhabitants of Matera cherish.

Serves 4

4 tablespoons extra virgin olive oil, plus a little extra to serve
3 cloves of garlic, chopped
1 dried red chilli, finely chopped
1 large onion, sliced
20 cherry tomatoes, halved
500g potatoes, peeled and cut into 2–4cm chunks
16 green or black olives
2 litres water
salt and freshly ground black pepper
750g *cime di rapa* or Swiss chard or purple sprouting broccoli, trimmed
4 eggs
200g stale good-quality bread, broken into chunks

To serve
freshly grated pecorino or Parmesan (optional)

Put the olive oil, garlic, chilli and onion into a roomy saucepan and place over a low-moderate heat. Fry gently until the onion is floppy and translucent. Add the tomatoes, stir around for a few seconds, then tip in the potatoes and olives. Pour in the water and season with salt and a little freshly ground black pepper. Bring up to the boil and simmer for 5 minutes.

Meanwhile, pile the greens up on your chopping board and slice thickly. Add to the saucepan, pressing them down into the liquid. Simmer for a further 10 minutes. Taste and add more salt if needed. Use the back of a ladle to make dips in the simmering pan of vegetables and break an egg into each one. Cover with a lid and let them poach for 4–5 minutes, until the whites are set.

Divide the chunks of bread between four bowls and carefully ladle the veg, the poached eggs and their broth over the top of them. Drizzle a little fresh olive oil over each bowl and serve with cheese for those that want it.

Il Ceccio Fritto

Fried Focaccia

Matera is famous, quite rightly, for its bread, which is excellent. I lust after one of the intricately carved wooden bread stamps that were once given as bridal gifts. They were used to identify the loaves of bread that each household sent to the communal bread ovens. Canny housewives kept a portion of the dough back to make *cecci fritti*, fried discs of dough that were served salted or, on special occasions, dipped in sugar or sweet fig syrup like doughnuts or *pettole* (see page 129). Modern Matera still cherishes its *cecci* and you can eat them with any number of different toppings in restaurants and *fritterie* (fry shops).

Serve them just as they are, plain and unadorned, or dress them up with tomatoes and oregano in the summer, or caramelised onions and chickpeas in colder months. If you have the time, leave the dough to rise slowly overnight in the fridge, then bring back to room temperature before using, to give it a little more flavour.

Makes 6

For the dough
350g strong white bread flour
10g salt
10g fresh yeast or 5g dried yeast
extra virgin olive oil
sunflower oil (optional)

Mix the flour with the salt and make a well in the centre. Pour in about 50ml of tepid water. Crumble in the yeast, then squidge it with your fingers to dissolve it into the water. Gradually mix in the flour, adding more tepid water as needed to make a soft dough (another 120–150ml should do it). Knead energetically for 10 minutes, until smooth and elastic. Form into a ball. Slurp a dash of olive oil into the mixing bowl and return the dough to the bowl, turning so that it is completely coated in oil. Cover the bowl with clingfilm and leave to rise until doubled in bulk.

Knead the dough again briefly, then divide into 6 pieces. Roll each one into a ball. One at a time, roll the balls of dough out thinly to form circles roughly 17–18cm in diameter, a few millimetres thick. Lay them out in a single layer on the work surface and cover with a damp tea towel (make sure you wring out every last drop of water first).

Shortly before eating, pour ½cm of olive oil (or a mix of sunflower and olive oil) into a wide frying pan. Place over a high heat. When the oil is hot, fry the *cecci* until golden brown on each side. Drain briefly on kitchen paper, sprinkle with a little salt, and serve naked, or topped generously with tomatoes or onions and chickpeas.

Tomato Topping

This is the classic topping for bruschetta or *frise* (bread rusks), but its vibrant freshness is a joy on a chewy mouthful of fried bread.

Serves 6

750g ripe tomatoes or cherry tomatoes
either 1–2 teaspoons dried oregano or a small handful
    of basil leaves, shredded, or both
a pinch or two of sugar (optional)
coarse sea salt flakes

freshly ground black pepper
extra virgin olive oil

If using full-size tomatoes, cut in half, deseed, then dice fairly small. If using cherry tomatoes, cut them in half or quarters, depending on size. Mix the tomatoes with the oregano or basil or both. If your tomatoes are a bit tart, add a pinch or two of sugar. Season to taste with salt, freshly ground black pepper and a good drizzle of olive oil. Use immediately, or set aside for half an hour or so for the flavours to meld.

Slow-cooked Onion and Chickpea Topping

My introduction to *cecci fritti* was at the Casino del Diavolo restaurant on Matera's outskirts. On top of the hot golden disc of dough was a gorgeous mess of onion and chickpeas. So damn good!

This is a great topping for bruschetta, as well. Toast slices of bread, rub with the cut side of half a clove of garlic and pile the mix on – they're a bit messy to eat, but that's what napkins are for.

Serves 6 generously

4 red or white onions, sliced
4 tablespoons extra virgin olive oil
3 bay leaves
5 parsley stalks
1 dried red chilli, finely chopped (optional)
salt and freshly ground black pepper
300g cooked chickpeas

Put the onions into a saucepan with all the remaining ingredients except the chickpeas. Place over a low heat, cover and leave to cook gently for around 20–30 minutes, stirring once or twice, until the onions are very tender. Remove the lid, add the chickpeas and cook together for another 4 or 5 minutes, until steamy and hot. Taste and adjust the seasoning. Discard the bay leaves and parsley stalks. Leave to cool if not using immediately. Reheat when needed.

Pettole Lucane or Crespelle Lucane or Grispelli Calabrese

Salty Savoury Doughnuts

Names collected so far for these excellent little (and sometimes large) savoury fritters: *pittule, pettole, crespelle, grispelli, ciambelline, culurielli, cuddruriaddri*. They exist in one form or another right along the south of Italy, from Puglian heel to Calabrian toe. The Puglian ones I've tasted have been softer – made with more refined flour – while the versions I've come across in Basilicata and Calabria have been chewier under their golden crust. High up in the hills of Calabria, I watched children weaving through the stalls of the town fair, pulling gleefully at the huge hoops of fried dough slung over their arms.

At Christmas and Easter and any other festive occasion, they may be tossed into sugar as they emerge from the sizzling fat, but I like them best plain, served hot and crisp, on their own alongside a glass of beer or red wine or as the doughy element in an *antipasto* table of little dishes.

They need to be eaten while they are still hot for the ultimate combination of crunch and chew, but if you can't contemplate the thought of deep-frying at the last minute, make them in advance and reheat them for 5 minutes or so on a baking tray in a medium-hot oven – around 180°C/160°C fan/gas 4.

Makes about 12

250g strong white bread flour
1 level teaspoon salt
200ml warm water
5g fresh yeast or 3g dried yeast

sunflower or vegetable oil for deep-frying
optional: caster sugar for the sweet version

Put the flour and salt into a relatively large bowl and make a well in the centre. Pour in a decent slurp of the water. Crumble in the fresh yeast, if using, or sprinkle in the dried yeast. Cream the yeast in the warm water with your fingers. Add the remaining water and mix with your fingers to form a wet dough. Work the dough for a good 10 minutes; scoop your hand round the edges of the bowl, pulling the dough up to stretch it and letting it fall back down again. Keep on going until the dough has developed a damp springiness. Clean your hands, cover the bowl with clingfilm or slide into a plastic bag and tuck the ends underneath. Set aside at room temperature for at least 6 hours, but a full 24 hours is far better – a long, lengthy prove produces a better flavour and a chewier texture.

Pour enough oil into a saucepan to give a depth of around 4cm. Place over a high heat. Pour a few extra tablespoons of oil into a bowl. Line a plate with a double layer of kitchen paper. Gather the plate, oil bowl and dough beside the hob.

Once the saucepan oil is good and hot, dip your fingers into the oil in the bowl and grab a small chunk of the dough (30–35g per fritter, though it's a bit tricky to weigh, so think of a glob of dough roughly the same size as a golf ball). Form into a vague ball, then stick a finger through the centre to produce the world's most uneven, most wobbly ring. Drop it into the hot oil. Repeat a few more times, dipping your fingers into oil to prevent the dough sticking.

Your mini-doughnuts will puff up swiftly – turn them once or twice and let them fry until a beautiful honey brown. Lift out and drain briefly on the kitchen paper. Repeat with the remaining dough. If you are after the sweet version, toss the *pettole* in caster sugar before serving. Otherwise, just serve them up swiftly.

It's a Roots Thing

High up in the hills of Basilicata, the wintertime is a bleak affair, with winds howling through empty streets and a cold that seeps into the bones. The views are breathtakingly beautiful, glimpsed, in my case, in haste as I search for the warmth of an isolated bar or restaurant. In my first visit there, in February, I missed the famous Carnevale of Tricarico which starts at an ungodly hour in the morning, with locals dressed in wild beribboned costumes representing the animals that were once herded across the hills. Two of the recommended restaurants I longed to visit were closed until Easter. I was too early for the Sagra della Rafanata at Marsico Nuovo. Thank heavens, then, for the cosy upstairs restaurant Pane e Lavore, in Rotondella. Genial staff and a glass of ruby-red Aglianico wine soothed away my frustration. Even better, this was where I finally got my first taste of *rafanata*.

La Rafanata is a surprising and moreish frittata of potatoes spiked with a tongue-tingling dose of freshly grated horseradish root. It is strongly associated with Carnevale, a festival that for all its supposed Christian fervour is so obviously an ancient, brief moment of respite in the darkest, harshest days of winter.

Horseradish grows wild in the Lucanian hills. Its characteristic zing of spiciness brings life and vigour to plain foods, so much so that it is often known here as '*il tartufo dei poveri*' – the poor person's truffle. And what a discovery! A grating of fresh horseradish root brings a plate of simple *pasta pomodoro* to life, imbuing a brilliant vigour. I am a total convert.

Years ago I cursed the plague of horseradish that flourished, no, invaded the corner of my small urban garden. There's only so much horseradish sauce a woman needs, I thought. Damn my predecessor who planted it there. If only I had realised its full potential I might have been more charitable. Nowadays, given that I wasn't about to scrabble around isolated Lucanian hilltops in an attempt to locate and dig up genuine wild horseradish from the hard, frost-bitten earth, I had to look elsewhere. Much as I love it, creamed horseradish (thank you Jill, who brought it over from the UK) is a far cry from the fieriness of the raw root. Eventually, an enterprising Puglian greengrocer tracked down a few roots for me, all the way from Germany. Two roots, as it turns out, go an awfully long way.

La Rafanata

Potato and Horseradish Frittata

I've cooked this frittata both with creamed horseradish straight from the jar and with freshly grated. They were both good, but the latter has a piquancy and tingle that makes it extra special. Either way, it is worth trying. If you want to use creamed horseradish, you'll need 80g and only 5 eggs.

As with many substantial *frittate*, this one can be cooked in a frying pan or in the oven. Serve your *rafanata* as part of an *antipasto*, or as a side dish with a bowl of steaming soup or a beautiful, dark beef stew.

Serves 6–8

1 large potato
6 medium eggs
80g freshly grated pecorino or Parmesan
50g freshly grated horseradish root
2 tablespoons finely chopped parsley
salt and freshly ground black pepper
2 tablespoons lard or extra virgin olive oil, plus extra for
    greasing

Peel the potato, cut into large chunks and boil until tender. Drain well, then mash. Weigh out 300g. Set aside until tepid, then beat in the eggs, pecorino or Parmesan, horseradish, parsley, salt and freshly ground black pepper. Fry a teaspoonful of the mixture in a little lard or olive oil to taste for seasoning. Add more horseradish, salt and/or black pepper as needed.

To bake: Preheat the oven to 200°C/180°C fan/gas 6. Grease a 23cm cake tin or baking dish generously with lard or olive oil.

Scrape in the mixture and smooth down. Bake for about 25–30 minutes, until just set – check the middle with the tip of a knife just in case there is still some liquid egg lurking under the crust. Serve warm or at room temperature, cut into wedges.

To fry: Preheat the grill. Return the frying pan to a lively heat, add the lard or olive oil, and get it spanking hot. Pour in the egg mixture. Stir briefly, then cook for a few minutes. Reduce the heat a little, cover with a lid and leave to cook for 3–4 minutes, until the underneath is browned, and the edges of the frittata are beginning to pull away from the sides of the pan. Slide the pan under the grill and cook until the top is set and patched with brown. Slide out on to a plate and eat warm or at room temperature, cut into wedges.

A note on buying and using fresh horseradish root

Fresh horseradish will, naturally, taste better and much hotter, not to mention more authentic, than the stuff from a glass jar, which tends to be sweetened and mollified. If you don't grow your own, you may occasionally notice it lurking around at a farmers' market or more rarely in a supermarket or greengrocers. Gardening manuals say that it should be harvested in the autumn, but you are far more likely to find it for sale in April, when demand is highest. Why? Because it's frequently eaten as part of the Jewish Passover feast, the seder, when a mouthful of eye-wateringly hot freshly grated horseradish represents the bitterness and harshness experienced by the Jewish people when they were enslaved by ancient Egyptian pharaohs.

Fresh horseradish is, potentially, a big blasting bomb of a root. Whole and rough and unworked it seems harmless enough. High-octane action happens the millisecond you start to peel away the rough outer skin. Enzymes hurtle into action to protect the root, instantly triggering the production of a chemical called allyl isothiocyanate. This is what we react to. Our sensory cells screech SOS messages to our brain. 'Help, help, we're under attack.' So we sneeze and snot and weep and sweat in an attempt to flush the enemy out of our system. Think onions, garlic, chilli, mustard, tear gas. Same reaction all round. The weirdest thing is that in small quantities this seems like a good idea. How very contrary our bodies are.

The point here, though, is that grating fresh horseradish will probably make you cry unless you a) fish out and wear the scuba goggles hidden at the bottom of the wardrobe, or b) use a food processor.

The good news is that the pungency of freshly grated horse-radish doesn't last long. This is also the bad news. Assuming you want the banging heat of horseradish to linger in your food, leave the whole grating business until the last minute.

Salsa di Cren

Italian Horseradish Sauce

I hesitated over including this recipe as it comes not from the south of Italy but from the opposite end of the country, traditionally served with the epic bollito misto (mixed cuts of meats simmered together in long, slow unison) of the Piedmont. Still, if you have a half root of horseradish left over from your *rafanata*, this is an excellent way of using some of it up. It has obvious similarities to both British bread sauce and horseradish sauce. Naturally it goes well with meats, particularly beef, but is perhaps even more appealing alongside grilled mackerel, smoked salmon or good cheese on toast.

Serves 8

40g freshly grated horseradish root
40g fresh breadcrumbs
2 tablespoons white wine vinegar
6 tablespoons extra virgin olive oil
1 teaspoon caster sugar
2 tablespoons water
salt

Mix everything together. If not using right away, spoon into a jar, smooth down, then cover the surface completely with a thin layer of olive oil. Seal and store in the fridge for up to a week.

Bourbonification

Say Bourbon and I think biscuit. I'm British and this seems like the only right-minded response. Peek Freans created the Creola biscuit in Bermondsey in 1910, rechristening it Bourbon two decades later. An American might reach for a shot glass anticipating a dram of Bourbon whiskey. A pastry chef will think vanilla, the best Bourbon vanilla. The French, however, leap beyond the stomach to the phenomenally powerful European House of Bourbon, which begat their kings Louis XIII to XVI. In Italy they might connect to the Borbone, the Spanish Bourbon rulers of the Kingdom of the Two Sicilies (which included Puglia, Basilicata and Calabria, as well as Naples) in the eighteenth and nineteenth centuries, distant right royal cousins of the French gang.

By all accounts the Spanish rulers were not universally popular with their Italian subjects. Riots and rebellions studded their reigns. I mentioned to an acquaintance in my local café on the corner of my street that I was researching the Borbone and he looked incredulous. 'Why? We got rid of them and don't want them back!' A long-inherited distrust apparently lingers on. They were eventually booted out by Garibaldi (another Peek Freans classic) and his Redshirts during the battles that led to Italian unification.

Their purported achievements and crimes can be debated endlessly, but their very presence in Italy shone a light on an important culinary corridor between Latin America and Italy. Take the *pignata* to *piñata* trail for instance. In Puglia, a *pignata* is the ubiquitous, traditional earthenware pot for long, slow cooking (more on page 180). You can pick up a handsome, fire-stained, pre-loved *pignata* relatively cheaply at one of the weekly antiques and bric-a-brac markets throughout the region, or a brand new factory-made one from a hardware store, or a brand new hand-thrown god of a *pignata* from a pottery studio.

Some time way back in the past, the odd habit of bashing a *pignata* to smithereens to get its cargo of seeds or dried fruit became associated with spring rituals, subsequently appropriated by the church. In Puglia, La Festa della Pentolaccia fell mid-Lent, when families hung their old damaged *pignatas* up, and whapped the hell out of them. The habit migrated gradually to Spain. Spanish conquistadors and the priests and monks who followed took the tradition across the Atlantic, integrating this jolly game into the Catholic mission. Gradually it took root, particularly in Mexico, and over the centuries the potentially dangerous clay pot has been replaced by increasingly fantastical card and paper creations.

Of course, the Spanish brought potatoes, tomatoes, corn and chillies back with them, too, eventually transforming the way we eat throughout Europe. In exchange, the Spanish gave Latin America limes and coriander. And disease and destruction; a fatal exchange indeed. Chocolate was another magnificent gift that travelled back to Europe with the tomatoes. The Mexican connection comes to the fore again in the handsome baroque town of Modica in the south of Sicily. Here they make a cold-worked dark chocolate that is, I believe, quite unique in Europe. Cocoa beans are ground to a paste on a *metate* hewn from the solidified lava stone that once flowed from Mount Etna. Volcanic stone *metate* have been used to grind corn and seeds in central America since long, long before the Spanish set foot in their 'new' world.

I'd like to imagine that there is another Latino-Spanish-southern Italian trail leading from the Mexican *pico de gallo salsa* (chopped tomato, onion, lime, chilli and coriander leaf) through to Spanish gazpacho and *salmorejo*, ground to a purée and enriched with olive oil, and on to the finely chopped summer salads I've eaten here, then up Italy to their more famous Tuscan compatriot, *panzanella*, a tomato and bread salad. Or perhaps I'm being fanciful. It may just be an entirely inevitable coincidence. When the summer heat beats down, what sane cook is going to stand over a hot fire when they could make a reinvigorating cooling salad from the vegetables and aromatics they just happen to have to hand?

There's no exact recipe for the southern Italian equivalents, but they all work along similar lines. In Matera, *cialledda fredda* (cold *cialledda* as opposed to the hot *cialledda calda*, see page 123) is a bread-based salad with tomato and red onion. It's known as the *colazione del mietitore*, the reapers' breakfast, eaten in the cool of early summer mornings before agricultural workers set out for the fields. In Calabria, they add a zip of chilli. In my home town of Ceglie Messapica, they mix tomatoes, celery, red onion and chunks of *frise* (double-baked bread rusk) to make *cialledda*. In other areas, it's known as *acquasale*, water-salt. My favourite version includes basil and oregano, and the ever-refreshing Puglian cucumber-melon, *carosele* or *baratiere*, as well. All are bathed in a mini-lake of water, creating a soupy salad to soothe parched throats on a steamy summer day.

Incidentally, Bourbon biscuits have no proper connection to the House of Bourbon. I dare say that even a century ago, the biscuit-naming committee at Peek Freans threw a lot of wild ideas around before arriving at a name which hinted at Bourneville chocolate, laced with a glamorous French-ish nod at royalty. Bourbon whiskey is said to have taken its name from either Bourbon County in Kentucky or the infamous Bourbon Street in New Orleans, both of which are named in honour of the French dynasty that supported the Americans in the War of Independence. Bourbon vanilla means vanilla grown on any one of a number of islands in the Indian Ocean. The French island of Réunion was originally christened the Isle Bourbon when it was annexed by Louis XIII in 1642. Here endeth the Bourbonic edibles history ramble. Thank you.

Acquasale

Vegetable and Bread Salad

Make your salad at least an hour before serving, allowing time for it to chill down and for the juices of the vegetables to flow and mingle. In my version, I've majored on the cooling quartet of tomato, cucumber-melon (or cucumber), celery and onion, piling them all on top of the stale bread just long enough before serving for it to soften but not go too soggy. For a more traditional *acquasale*, double the quantity of bread, break it into rough bits and mix it with the rest from the get-go.

Serves 6

a handful of basil leaves
300g cherry tomatoes, halved or quartered if large
2 stems of celery, diced
150g *carosella*, *barratiere* or cucumber, deseeded and
    peeled if necessary, diced
3 tablespoons extra virgin olive oil, plus a little extra for
    serving
1 tablespoon capers, rinsed thoroughly if salted
½ a red onion, finely diced
½ tablespoon dried oregano
½ tablespoon red wine vinegar
salt and freshly ground black pepper
2 slices of stale high-quality bread

Reserve a few of the basil leaves for garnishing. Shred the rest and mix with all the remaining ingredients except the bread. Stir in 200ml of water. Cover and chill for at least an hour. Stir and adjust the seasoning – you may well need a dash more vinegar, or extra salt. Lay the bread in a single layer in a shallow serving dish and pile the acquasale and all its juices over it. Let it stand for a couple of minutes to allow the bread to soften. Serve lightly chilled, with a fine drizzle of fresh olive oil over the top, and scattered with the reserved basil leaves.

Insalata di Arance, Finocchi e Olive

Orange, Fennel and Black Olive Salad

I've loved this salad for as long as I can remember. My mum used to make it way, way back and I guess she probably came across the combination even way-er back when she travelled around Italy in the '50s. Nibble on a scrap of orange before you dress the salad. If it is super sweet, be generous with the lemon juice. If it is a tad on the sharp side, be restrained with the lemon – you'll need just enough to lift the flavour of the fennel.

Serves 4

1 orange, peeled and fairly thinly sliced
1 or 2 fennel bulbs, depending on size, trimmed and very
    thinly sliced
a few squeezes of lemon juice
2 tablespoons extra virgin olive oil
salt and freshly ground black pepper
a handful of black olives
a little chopped parsley or a handful of basil leaves

Arrange/mix the orange and fennel on a serving plate. Squeeze over the lemon juice, drizzle with the olive oil and season with salt and freshly ground black pepper. Scatter over the olives and the parsley or basil, and serve.

Pane e Lavoro's Mortadella alla Piastra

Seared Mortadella with Pistachios and Balsamic Vinegar

Tucked away in the backstreets of Rotondella, a town that clings in tight spirals around its hilltop, is the excellent restaurant Pane e Lavoro. Thank heavens, because there was nowhere else to eat on the two icy nights I lodged there. It takes its name from the stories the owner's grandfather told him of the grim years of the early twentieth century, when bread prices rose way beyond the purses of the poor of Italy. In Basilicata, bread, not pasta, was still the mainstay of the diet, supported by vegetables and pulses. Desperate times and empty stomachs led to riots, propelled by shouts of '*Pane e lavoro!*' – bread and work.

Though mortadella is now a commonplace deli sausage throughout Italy, thinly sliced for sandwiches and as *antipasto* or sold in a chunk for cooking, it hails originally from Bologna, where it was an expensive luxury for the rich. Six hundred years ago, grinding meat, fat and spices to the smoothest of smooth pastes with a pestle and mortar demanded intense labour and lots of time. Nowadays it's accomplished in minutes by clanking giants of metal, extruding perfect bulging logs of mortadella for the supermarkets.

Speedily seared mortadella is a revelation. Heat transforms it into something remarkably delicious, a dish of such exquisite and unexpected simplicity. Ignore the stuff in packets and head straight to the deli counter to request one chunky slice of mortadella, cut around ½cm thick.

Serves 4–6, as a starter or part of an *antipasto*

1 thick slice of mortadella, weighing around 240g
a little extra virgin olive oil
4 heaped teaspoons chopped pistachios
2 tablespoons balsamic vinegar

To serve (optional)
a few handfuls of rocket or watercress

Put a heavy-based frying pan over a high heat. Arrange a bed of rocket or watercress on each plate if using. Cut the mortadella into 12 wedges and brush one side only with olive oil. Lay half the wedges, oil side down, in the frying pan. Sear for a minute or two until golden brown underneath, then turn over and do the same on the other side.

Whip this first lot of browned mortadella out of the pan and replace with the second batch, cooking them as above. Arrange the cooked wedges on the green leaves, or on a single serving plate. Top each wedge with a layer of finely chopped pistachios (be generous), then drizzle, also generously, with balsamic vinegar. Repeat with the remaining cooked wedges and serve swiftly while still warm.

La Crapiata

Matera's Bean and Grain Soup

There can be few dishes that give so much for so little. *La Crapiata* is tasty, nutritious, vegan, hugely satisfying, cheap, and above all brings the gift of scatological/lavatorial mirth to the tables of English speakers. In short, a perfect family recipe.

La Crapiata is a sturdy sludge of a soup/stew that has its origins in the cave slums of Matera. You might imagine that it is a winter dish, boiled up to stave off the icy *tramontana* winds that whistle around the town in the cold months, but you would be wrong. It's a summer celebration dish and more of a concept than an exact recipe.

In early August, once the harvest was all safely gathered in, after all that back-breaking work under sweltering summer sun, neighbours would take a break together to party modestly with *la crapiata*, their harvest supper. This was the time to finish off the last scraps of dried beans and vegetables from the year before. Every family contributed, with a handful of dried chickpeas here a few dried fava beans there, lentils and *cicerchie* (another local legume), dried whole grains of wheat and whatever else was lurking at the back of the cupboards. Into the cauldron with them all, together with the last of the old crop of potatoes and carrots, a few stems of celery. A seasoning of the summer's ripe red tomatoes joined them. That's it. Just water and salt to add to the mix and a couple of long hours of simmering until the beans and potatoes begin to dissolve, leaving the ivory wheat bobbling in the purée.

When I make it I like to make sure there are dried borlotti beans in the mix, split dried broad beans (*fave*) if I have them and a few chickpeas, but honestly the point is that you need a variety of diverse pulses. The wheat is the one essential unchallengeable ingredient. It's a great way to clear out the ends of packs of dried beans lurking in the back of the kitchen cupboard. Failing that, a packet of mixed beans straight from the wholefood shop or the supermarket will do well. Make it your own but make it in the winter, not on a sweltering hot summer's day.

Serves 8

500g dried beans
100g dried green or brown lentils
100g dried whole wheat berries
500g potatoes, peeled and roughly chunked
2 carrots, thickly sliced
1 onion, roughly chopped
2 stems of celery, sliced
3 bay leaves
2 sprigs of rosemary or 3 sprigs of thyme
2–3 dried red chillies
250g tomatoes, roughly chopped
6 cloves of garlic, roughly chopped
salt and freshly ground black pepper
extra virgin olive oil

Soak the beans, lentils and wheat berries together in plenty of cold water overnight. Drain and tip into a large saucepan or casserole dish. Add all the remaining ingredients, except the olive oil. Add enough water to cover by around 6cm. It's fine to add a good helping of salt at this stage, by the way.

Bring up to the boil, then turn the heat down and cover with a lid, leaving a small gap for steam to escape. Simmer gently for 1½–2 hours, until you have a thick, gloopy sludge. You'll need to stir occasionally at first, more frequently as the soup thickens to prevent it catching and burning on the base of the pan. By now the lentils, potatoes and much of the beans will have broken down, leaving just the wheat and a few larger bits of bean to add texture. Taste and adjust the seasoning, and serve hot and steaming with a drizzle of olive oil over each bowlful.

Falagoni Lucani

Lucanian Pasties

Falagoni are Basilicata's ultimate portable meal, big enough to satisfy, small enough to slide into a pocket. Like the Cornish pasty or Latin American *empanada*, they are everyman food, with fillings based on plentiful, cheap local produce, wrapped in a half-moon package of pastry. Most are filled with vegetables in one form or another, with a local variation here and a family twist there. The simplest are the best, I think. Plain Swiss chard, seasoned with a little garlic and chilli, is seriously good. My friend Francesco's mother, Filomena, throws a handful of raisins in among the greens and that's even better. Potato, onion and cheese is more robust, while summery courgettes make for a lighter, fresher filling.

Lard gives the pastry a more tender, shorter crumb, excellent hot from the oven. The olive-oil-based pastry emerges from the oven crisp and hard, but softens a little as it cools, making it the better option when you want to take the pasties out for a picnic or a packed lunch.

Makes 6

For the pastry
300g 00 flour or plain flour, plus extra for rolling out
¼ teaspoon salt
1 egg
either 60g lard or 3 tablespoons extra virgin olive oil

For the filling
350g Swiss chard
salt

1 clove of garlic, thinly sliced
1 fresh red chilli, deseeded and finely chopped
45g sultanas or raisins (optional)
1 tablespoon extra virgin olive oil

To glaze
1 egg yolk
1 tablespoon milk

Begin with the filling. Rinse the Swiss chard and dry it as best you can on kitchen paper or a clean tea towel. Pile it up on your chopping board and slash it into 1cm wide ribbons. Tip into a colander set over a bowl and sprinkle with 1 level tablespoon salt. Mix well, then leave to drain for at least half an hour, turning occasionally if you remember. Shortly before using, squeeze firmly to eliminate a few more drops of moisture, then mix with the garlic, chilli, sultanas or raisins if using, and the olive oil.

Now that pastry. Mix the flour with the salt and make a well in the centre. Break in the egg and add the lard or olive oil. Work the lard/liquids together with your fingers, gradually bringing in the flour. Add just enough water to form a soft dough – around 5–6 tablespoons. Knead briefly, roll into a ball, wrap in clingfilm and leave to rest at room temperature for half an hour or so.

Preheat the oven to 180°C/160°C fan/gas 4. Divide the dough into 6 portions. Roll each one out to form a 20cm circle (more or less – perfection is not required here). Spoon a sixth of the filling on to one side of the pastry, leaving a clean 2cm border all round. Fold the pastry over to form a semi-circle. Press the edges together firmly. Working your way gradually around the border, fold the edge over on itself and press down to ensure that the filling is firmly enclosed. Lay the pasties on a baking tray lined with baking parchment. Mix the egg yolk and milk for the glaze and brush over the pasties.

Prick the tops all over with a cocktail stick or a fork to allow steam to escape as the pasties cook. Bake for 30 minutes, until golden brown. Serve warm or at room temperature.

Potato, Cheese and Onion Filling

> 400g potatoes, peeled
> 1½ onions, halved and very thinly sliced
> salt and freshly ground black pepper
> 45g freshly grated pecorino or Parmesan
> 1 tablespoon extra virgin olive oil

Using a vegetable peeler or a mandoline, slice the potatoes paper thin. Mix with the onion and some salt and tip into a colander. Leave to drain for at least half an hour. Shortly before using, squeeze hard to expel the moisture, then mix with the grated cheese, olive oil and lots of freshly ground black pepper.

Courgette, Onion and Pecorino Filling

> 500g courgettes
> 1 onion, halved and very thinly sliced
> salt and freshly ground black pepper
> 1 clove of garlic, crushed
> 2 eggs
> 25g freshly grated pecorino or Parmesan
> 20g dried breadcrumbs

Slice the courgettes thinly. Mix with the onion and some salt and scrape into a colander set over a bowl. Leave for at least half an hour. Squeeze firmly to expel as much water as possible. Tip into a bowl and mix with the garlic, eggs, cheese, breadcrumbs and plenty of freshly ground black pepper.

U Pastizz R'Tunnar

Rotondella's Pork Pasties

In the town of Rotondella, the *falagon* becomes the *pastizz*, a pasty filled with meat, originally for high days and holidays, particularly Easter, the annual pilgrimage to the Sanctuary of Santa Maria d'Anglona in September and on the occasion of the annual pig slaughter in the late autumn. That was when meat was a rare, impossibly extravagant treat. Nowadays, you can eat them any time of year in local bars and restaurants or even grab a box of freezer-ready *pastizz* to go home with you. The Sagra ru Pastizz is celebrated in high summer, a feast of pasties washed down with plenty of wine, beer and some lively dancing.

Like *falagoni*, the pastry is crisp and hard when it emerges from the oven, then softens a little in the best of ways when left overnight, wrapped in a clean tea towel. Though pork is widely used for the filling, lamb is a popular alternative, particularly around Easter.

Makes 6

1 quantity *falagoni* pastry (page 148)

For the filling
500g lean pork, cut into 2–3cm cubes
1 egg
30g freshly grated pecorino
2 tablespoons extra virgin olive oil
2 tablespoons chopped parsley
salt

To glaze
1 egg yolk
1 tablespoon milk

For the filling, mix the pork with the egg, pecorino, olive oil, parsley and a pinch or two of salt, but no more than that as the cheese is already pretty salty.

Preheat the oven to 180°C/160°C fan/gas 4. Divide the dough into 6 portions. Roll each one out to form a 20cm circle (more or less – perfection is not required here). Spoon a sixth of the filling on to the pastry, slightly off centre, but leaving a clean 2cm border all round. Fold the pastry over to form a semi-circle. Press the edges together firmly. Working your way gradually around the border, fold the edge over on itself and press down to ensure that the filling is firmly enclosed. Lay the pasties on a baking tray lined with baking parchment. Mix the egg yolk and milk for the glaze and brush over the pasties.

Prick the tops all over with a cocktail stick or a fork to allow steam to escape as the pasties cook. Bake for 30 minutes, until golden brown. Serve warm or at room temperature.

Spaghetti alla San Giuannin

Spaghetti with Anchovy, Olives, Capers and Chilli

San Giuannin is a Materan dialect name for San Giovanni or St John, whose saint's day is celebrated on June 24th. His very own spaghetti dish bears an uncanny resemblance to Neapolitan *spaghetti puttanesca*, the whore's spaghetti, garnished with a halo of holiness. There is, perhaps, a little less tomato in it, but the glorious salty, umami-rich, spicy lick of flavour is pretty much identical. Whatever you call it, this is one of the simpler and most satisfying of spaghetti dishes, and one that graces tables throughout southern Italy particularly in the summer months.

Serves 4

350–400g spaghetti or *tagliolini*
salt
4 tablespoons extra virgin olive oil
3 or 4 cloves of garlic, chopped
6 anchovy fillets
1 or 2 red chillies, fresh or dried, finely chopped
125g cherry tomatoes, halved
2 tablespoons capers, rinsed thoroughly if salted
120g black olives, stoned
3 tablespoons chopped parsley

To serve
freshly grated Parmesan

Cook the spaghetti or *tagliolini* in plenty of salted boiling water.

Make the sauce while the pasta cooks. Put the olive oil, garlic, anchovies and chillies into a wide frying pan, place over a moderate heat, and fry, mashing the anchovies into the oil, until the garlic begins to colour. Add the halved cherry tomatoes. Cover and let it cook for a couple of minutes. Remove the lid, and add the capers, olives and most of the parsley (save a little for garnishing). Stir them in, then add a ladleful of the cooking water from the pan of pasta. Let it cook down for a minute or so more.

By now, the pasta should be al dente. Scoop out a mugful of the water and set aside, then drain the pasta. Tip it into the frying pan and toss with the sauce, adding a slurp or two of the reserved cooking water to help the sauce coat the pasta lightly. Serve immediately, with freshly grated Parmesan.

Baccalà

The Portuguese claim the prize for eating the most salt cod in the world – a whopping 35kg per person per annum. Italy lags behind, but it puts in a spirited attempt. *Baccalà* is not the stuff of everyday meals but it is much appreciated, especially throughout the winter months. It owes its popularity in part to bishops, in part to convenience, and in part to geography. And of course, it tastes damn good too.

When the early Catholic bishops congregated for the Council of Nicaea in the fourth century and later medieval clerics argued their way through the Council of Trent, among other hugely important decrees they codified the need for fast days, particularly on Fridays, the day Jesus died, and particularly throughout Lent. Fasting meant not eating the flesh of warm-blooded beasts. Cold-blooded creatures like fish, on the other hand, were fine.

In pre-refrigeration days, fresh fish may have been plentiful all along the coast but it just didn't travel. There was no way fresh fish could remain fresh when it was loaded on to a donkey to trek slowly inland along rough roads and steep hillsides. Both poor and wealthy were deprived of fresh fish unless a nearby stream could provide. Scandinavian dried salt cod, durable and comparatively light, proved a neat solution to erstwhile fishless Fridays. Hurrah! Thank you, redoubtable Vikings and fearless big-sea fishermen. Eons later, *baccalà*, salt cod, still holds a strong position on southern Italian tables. Not every day, not even every week – the good stuff is expensive, especially when you buy it presoaked – but for a treat and a celebration. It's an essential component in the big fishy Christmas Eve meal with all the family gathered around the table.

Salting and drying works a quiet transformation on cod in much the same way as it turns raw pork into *prosciutto crudo*.

The flavour is more rounded and perhaps a little sweeter. The texture firmer and a tad chewier. Mostly I really like salt cod. Sometimes I don't (when it is still too salty, or when it has been overcooked to a fibrous blob in a watery sauce). These things are totally avoidable and that starts with planning ahead.

Buying, preparing and cooking salt cod

If you live in Italy or Spain or Portugal, you will be able to buy salt cod with ease from local shops or from the supermarket, particularly in the colder months and even more particularly in the run-up to Christmas. Elsewhere it is more of a challenge. Some fishmongers stock it in the UK and it may be available in Caribbean food shops too. Track it down and then be choosy. The best cut is from the shoulder of the fish, where the flesh is thickest. The dried fish should be pale yellow and firm. The smell is noticeable, as you might expect from dried fish, but not unpleasant and it definitely shouldn't be tainted with mould or rot.

To rehydrate and desalinate the fish, start by rinsing off the surface salt under the cold tap. Now soak it in cold water in the fridge for at least 24 hours if the flesh is fairly thin, better 48 hours for thicker prime pieces. Change the water twice a day or more. Taste a small strip from the thickest part to make sure that it is palatable (it's actually rather delicious raw) before cooking. If it is still too salty, soak for a few more hours in fresh cold water.

In many recipes, you can move straight on to poaching the fish, removing the skin and bones afterwards. For the four that follow here, however, you will have to remove the skin and bones from the raw soaked cod and this demands a degree of determination. Grasp a corner of the skin and tease it away from the flesh until you can get a good grasp. With the help of a knife, tug the skin off little by little, scraping down the shreds of flesh as you work. Next feel for the bones. Use a sharp knife to cut them out. And with that it is ready for the next stage.

Baccalà is either poached or fried. When poaching, either in water or milk or directly in a sauce, keep the heat low so that it just poaches gently. Do not let the liquid boil hard or you will end up with stringy, over-wrought fish. In an apparently contradictory manner, fried *baccalà* demands a high heat to produce a crisp exterior, but it is important to protect it first, either by simply but comprehensively tossing in flour, or dipping in batter or coating in breadcrumbs.

Insalata di Baccalà Crudo

Raw Salt Cod Salad

They do it in Barcelona and they do it in Basilicata. In those hot summer months, salt cod salads make sense. Soaked into mildness, raw salt cod is unexpectedly delicious. Add sweet sharp tomatoes, olive oil and a dab of garlic and you have the perfect light lunch or *antipasto*.

Serves 6 as an *antipasto*, 3–4 as a main course

150g dried salt cod, soaked, or 250g pre-soaked salt cod
350g cherry tomatoes, halved, or ripe sweet full-size
    tomatoes, deseeded and diced
¼ of a red onion, chopped
1 tablespoon red wine vinegar
1–2 tablespoons lemon juice
4 tablespoons extra virgin olive oil
1 clove of garlic, crushed
a handful of basil leaves, plus a few extra to garnish
salt and freshly ground black pepper

Remove the skin and bones from the soaked cod, then cut it into cubes. Toss with all the remaining ingredients, going lightly on the salt. Let the salad marinate in the fridge for an hour or two. Taste and adjust the seasoning, and scatter a few fresh basil leaves over the top before serving.

Baccalà con Pomodoro e Olive

Salt Cod with Cherry Tomatoes and Green Olives

The neat thing here is that the cod is poached in no more than a mess of cherry tomatoes and its own juices, which ooze out and combine to produce a little lake of sauce. This makes it absolutely imperative that your *baccalà* is totally, thoroughly and comprehensively soaked. Get that right and you have a wonderfully southern Italian take on salt cod.

Serves 4–6

500g dried salt cod, soaked, or 700g pre-soaked
    salt cod
3 tablespoons extra virgin olive oil
1 red onion, chopped
2 cloves of garlic, finely chopped
1 dried red chilli, finely chopped
300g cherry tomatoes
a good handful of basil leaves, plus a few extra to finish
100g green olives
salt and freshly ground black pepper

Remove the skin and bones from the soaked cod. Cut the fish into chunky pieces, around 6cm across.

Put the olive oil into a frying pan with the onion, garlic and chilli. Cook over a gentle heat, stirring occasionally, until the onion is tender and translucent. Add the tomatoes and most of the basil leaves, setting a few aside to garnish. Season with freshly ground black pepper but NO SALT. Stir, then cover and leave to cook for 10 minutes, stirring again once or twice.

Now nestle the pieces of cod into the tomato sauce and scatter the olives among them. Cover the pan and let it simmer for another 10 minutes. Turn the pieces of cod over and stir the juices into the tomato goo, then cover again and cook for a final 5–10 minutes, until the cod flakes easily. Taste the sauce and adjust the seasoning, adding salt if needed. Garnish with the remaining basil leaves and serve.

Baccalà con Pomodoro, Olive e Sultanina

Salt Cod with Tomatoes, Olives and Sultanas

This is a great combination of crisp fried salt cod with a rich tomato sauce speckled with salty olives and sweet sultanas. The sauce can be made in advance and reheated, but don't fry the cod until the last possible minute.

Serves 4

500g dried salt cod, soaked, or 700g pre-soaked salt
    cod
4 tablespoons extra virgin olive oil
1 onion, chopped
3 cloves of garlic, chopped
1 x 400g tin of chopped tomatoes
2 generous tablespoons tomato purée
2 tablespoons chopped parsley
salt and freshly ground black pepper
50g sultanas or raisins
100g black olives, stoned
plain flour

Remove the skin and bones from the soaked cod. Cut the flesh into chunky cubes, around 4–5cm across.

To make the sauce, put 2 tablespoons of olive oil into a frying pan with the onion and garlic. Set over a gentle heat and cook for at least 10 minutes, stirring occasionally, until the onion is soft and golden. Now add the tomatoes, tomato purée, most of the parsley (save a little for garnishing), a little salt and lots of freshly ground black pepper. Add about 100ml of water, too. Stir, then simmer for 15–20 minutes, until very thick. Stir in the sultanas or raisins and olives, then taste and adjust the seasoning. Cool if not using immediately.

Ten minutes or so before you want to sit down to eat, toss the *baccalà* in plenty of flour. Heat 2 tablespoons of olive oil in a clean frying pan over a moderately-high heat. Fry the floured pieces of cod, turning occasionally, until golden brown. Reheat the sauce and spoon into a serving dish or on to individual plates. Arrange the hot fried *baccalà* on top, scatter with the remaining parsley and serve.

Baccalà Fritto con Cipolle e Ceci

Fried Salt Cod with Onions and Chickpeas

Throughout the area, particularly cherished combinations of foodstuffs are repeated in different combinations, and this recipe is a clear example. Golden-brown fried salt cod as in the previous recipe is just terrific served with the sweet-savoury mix of onions and chickpeas from page 128.

Serves 4

500g dried salt cod or 750g pre-soaked salt cod
plain flour
2 tablespoons extra virgin olive oil
1 quantity Slow-cooked Onion and Chickpea Topping
  (page 128)
a little chopped parsley

Remove the skin and bones from the soaked cod. Cut the flesh into chunky cubes, around 4–5cm across.

Ten minutes or so before you want to sit down to eat, toss the *baccalà* in plenty of flour. Heat the olive oil in a frying pan over a moderately-high heat, and fry the floured pieces of cod, turning occasionally, until golden brown. Reheat the onions and chick-peas and spoon into a serving dish or on to individual plates. Arrange the hot fried *baccalà* on top, scatter with chopped parsley and serve.

Call Me by My Names

For a region that is often considered a slow, out-of-the-way backwater, Basilicata has quite the wild bellicose history, full of lustful warfare. It also has something of an identity crisis: is it really Basilicata, or is it actually Lucania? Does it matter? Probably not.

In the beginning, the Oenotrian and Choni tribes lived among the mountains and valleys. Then in the fifth century BC, the aggressive Lucani, warriors and conquerors to a man, galloped in, grasping control and settling themselves comfortably into their new territories between the Adriatic and the Gulf of Taranto. There they stayed for centuries, still skirmishing and squabbling with other tribes but clearly marking Lucania as their territory. Until, of course, the Roman armies turned up and wiped the floor with them.

Leap forward another millennium, and now the Lucanian lands are part of the Byzantine Empire. This is when it was rechristened Basilicata, from the Greek word *basilikós*, belonging to a king. Leap on again, almost another millennium, to 1932. Now it is Mussolini's turn to meddle. Basilicata was abandoned, Lucania reinstated. A mere hop and a skip on to 1947: the post-war government restored the name Basilicata and so it has remained, officially at least, until the present day.

The curious thing is that despite all, the locals use the two names interchangeably, marginally favouring Lucania over Basilicata. I understand the pull of the older name. It carries a sense of rootedness in the land, independence, a territorial belonging, whereas Basilicata demotes them to a mere trinket in the jewelbox of a long-gone empire.

Metapontino, Saracens and Oranges

The Ionian coast of Basilicata sweeps for some forty kilometres around the edge of the Gulf of Taranto. The long sandy beaches are beautiful, punctuated every now and then with holiday resorts, marinas and fishing boats. Turn your back to the sea and gaze inland, and you see the flat expanse of the Metapontino plain. It's not the most exciting of landscapes but it is fertile and hugely productive. It was once a place of swamps and marshes and malaria, but throughout the last century, land reclamation initiatives transformed it into a vast market garden. A fair amount of the fresh fruit and vegetables that I buy in my local market will have been trucked in from this patchwork of fields.

The town of Policoro is famous for its sweet strawberries. There's fennel and tomatoes and peppers and asparagus aplenty. Apricots, peaches, plums and pomegranates proliferate. Above all, though, it is known for its citrus fruit, and of these, by far the most romantic is Tursi's orange, the *arancia staccia*.

This orange does not make it to my market. The orchards that surround the town and its neighbour Montalbano Jonico have a limited production, just enough to supply the locale. It is sweet, seedless, thick-peeled, juicy and BIG. Your average orange weighs in at around 140g, but a '*stacc*' breaks the scales at around 300g and more. Grapefruit size, then. In a world where the convenience of clementines and mandarins is highly rated, I can see that it doesn't really make broader commercial sense.

The local legend tells us that the orange was introduced by the Saracens who made their home here in the ninth century. A short tenure that left a lasting impression. They settled high up at the top of the steep hill. This oldest part of Tursi is still known as La Rabatana, taking its name from the Arabic word for a base or fortification. Over the centuries, Rabatana flourished, then declined. Now the narrow streets and crumbling houses are home to just a handful of families. It is a village of ghosts, chased by winds swirling through the alleys.

From the heights of Rabatana, the view across the plain of Metapontino to the sea is breathtaking. Down below, the orange groves are verdant and lush. I love the legend of the 'stacc', even though it seems unlikely. Sweet oranges weren't introduced to Europe for another half a millennium. Never mind, the connection is strong and the lucky inhabitants of the towns are right to celebrate this rare and beautiful citrus fruit.

Pesce San Pietro al Forno con Asparagi, Olive e Arance

Roast John Dory (or Sea Bream) with Asparagus, Orange and Olives

A recipe for when you spot sparkling fresh fish in the spring-time. John Dory are easily recognisable by the black 'thumb-print' on each side. Myth has it that this was imprinted for ever by the hand of St Peter as he pulled the fish out of the sea. The recipe works well with sea bream, too.

Here there's a nice serendipity: the last of the winter's oranges linger on the market as the first asparagus comes in, and they work so well together.

Serves 4

1 orange
2 John Dory, weighing about 700g–1kg each, or 2 sea
    bream, cleaned
3 tablespoons extra virgin olive oil
500g asparagus, trimmed
a handful of basil leaves
salt and freshly ground black pepper
75g black olives

Preheat the oven to 220°C/200°C fan/gas 7. Peel the zest off the orange with a vegetable peeler. Cut a third into very fine shreds. Blanch in boiling water for 2 minutes, then drain. Tuck the remaining zest inside the fish. Squeeze out the orange juice. Make a couple of deep slashes across the thicker part of each side of each fish.

Spoon 2 tablespoons of olive oil into a large baking dish or roasting tin. Add the asparagus and most of the basil leaves (save a few to garnish), season with salt, and roll them around until they are evenly coated in oil. Push them to the sides, without overlapping too much, and lay the fish in the middle. Scatter the olives over the asparagus. Brush the fish with the remaining oil, then drizzle the orange juice over both fish and the asparagus. Scatter over the blanched orange zest. Season with salt and freshly ground black pepper.

Roast for 20 minutes, until the John Dory is just cooked through. Dot with the reserved basil leaves and serve.

Coniglio alla Cacciatora

Rabbit with White Wine and Mushrooms

I was once given a very good recipe for chicken cacciatora by a taxi driver in Sicily. This is not it. And not only because it starts with a rabbit. The thing about huntsman's wife's chicken/rabbit is that it is not a formula set in Italian marble. A quick trawl through the internet brings up dozens of different versions, here with mushrooms, there with a ton of tomatoes, some with capers, here with white wine, there with red, most with olives, mostly green but sometimes black. This then is my version and I make no claims to authenticity. It starts with a whole rabbit, but if that is just too much to bear, use a chicken instead.

Down here in the south, rabbit cacciatora will be served after the pasta course with very little in the way of accompaniments. Being a foreigner, I have no qualms about serving it with plenty of polenta or a pile of buttery mashed potato, together with lightly blanched, al dente greens of some sort. When I presented Paola, a local friend, with this she raved delightedly about the mashed potato – so not a thing down here – but tut-tutted firmly about the crisp-hearted green beans, declaring them sweetly, but firmly, *molto* or undercooked. There's no pleasing everyone.

Serves 4–6

1 rabbit, skinned and cleaned

For the rabbit stock
2 tablespoons extra virgin olive oil
1 onion, diced

1 carrot, diced
1 stem of celery, thinly sliced
2 cloves of garlic, sliced
1 sprig of rosemary
2 sprigs of thyme
2 sprigs of myrtle (optional)
2 parsley stalks
1 bay leaf
10 black peppercorns
150ml dry white wine

For the stew proper
3 tablespoons extra virgin olive oil, plus an extra dash
250g *cardoncelli* (king oyster) mushrooms (or use
    portobello mushrooms), sliced
½ an onion, chopped
120g smoked pancetta, cut into lardons
2 cloves of garlic, chopped
150ml dry white wine
2 tablespoons plain flour
2 tablespoons tomato purée
salt and freshly ground black pepper
100g stoned black or green olives
2 tablespoons capers, rinsed thoroughly if salted
a little chopped parsley, to garnish

Part 1: A spot of butchery — make sure you sharpen your knife first

The first thing to do is to separate the tastiest, meatiest bits of rabbit from all the rest, that's the thighs and the saddle. If the head is still in situ, cut it off at the top of the neck and get rid of it — I'm not squeamish but I'd really prefer not to have those big eyes staring at me as I hack the body up.

Next slash the meat at the base of the thighs so that they are loose enough to bend back, away from the main body, snapping the thigh bone out of its socket. Now you can easily cut them off. Reserve on the meaty pile. Cut off the forearms in the same way, but use these to start the stock pile.

If they are included, remove the liver, heart, kidneys and any other organs from the central cavity. Keep the liver and the kidneys on the meaty pile, the heart on the stock pile. Discard the rest. The front end of the torso is basically just skin and bones. Cut it off just above where the meaty part starts and add those to the stock pile. Carefully cut along the backbone on either side, drawing the knife downwards, against the bone, to loosen the saddle parts. Cut away any rib bones to release the prize saddle joints. These, of course, go on the meaty pile. Wrap them up and pop them back in the fridge until needed.

Part 2: The stock

Put the olive oil into a saucepan with the diced onion and carrot, the sliced celery and garlic and the stock pile of bones. Cook over a high heat for 5–10 minutes, turning the veg and bones every couple of minutes. The idea is to get a bit of brown on the veg and here and there on the bones, but don't let them burn. Add the herbs and the peppercorns, then pour over the wine. Let it sizzle for a minute or so, then pour in 750ml of water. Bring up to the boil, half cover the pan, then simmer for at least 1 hour, stirring occasionally. If time is with you, keep on cooking for longer, adding a little more water as needed. Leave to cool, then strain out the solids and reserve the stock. If time is on your side, go through the debris and strip the shreds of meat off. These can either be added to the final *cacciatora* or used in a completely new dish, anything from a rabbit and potato hash to a burly rabbit and red wine risotto.

Part 3: The stew proper

Heat 2 tablespoons of olive oil in a frying pan over a high heat. Add the mushrooms and sauté briskly until patched with brown and tender. Scoop out and reserve. Add the large chunks of rabbit, liver and kidneys from the meaty pile to the pan, with a dash more oil if needed, and brown on all sides. Lift out on to a plate. Wipe the frying pan out with kitchen paper and return it to the hob, over a much lower heat. Spoon in the last of the oil, and add the chopped half onion and the pancetta. Fry gently until the onion is tender and translucent. Add the garlic and cook for 30 seconds or so to soften. Pour in the wine and let it sizzle away until almost all evaporated. Sprinkle over the flour and stir to mix in evenly. Gradually stir in the stock, the tomato purée, salt and freshly ground black pepper. Return the rabbit thighs only to the pan. Half cover and leave to simmer for 30 minutes, stirring and turning the thighs occasionally. By now the liquid should have thickened enough to make a decent sauce.

While the thighs simmer, slice the saddle meat thickly. Add it to the pan along with the liver, kidneys, mushrooms, olives and capers. Simmer for another 5 minutes, then taste and adjust the seasoning. Serve sprinkled with a little chopped parsley.

More Than Crisp

Launched on the world in 1954 (thank you, Henry Walker) the cheese and onion crisp has embedded itself in the British taste pantheon, topping the polls for decades. Over in America, the best seller by a mile is the plain chip. Italy is pretty much in line with America. Crisps here tend to be dull and, in bars at any rate, slightly stale. I did notice big bags of truffle-flavoured crisps in a deli near me recently, but flavoured crisps do not have much of a presence.

Basilicata, however, has obliterated the whole crisp issue with its own, fabulous alternative – *peperoni cruschi*, fried sun-dried red peppers. If burrata is Puglia's gift to the world, *'nduja* Calabria's, then *peperoni cruschi* are Basilicata's, though the world hasn't caught on yet. I can think of no better accompaniment to an ice-cold glass of beer or white wine or aperol spritz on a hot summer's day, than a plate piled with glossy, bulls' blood red, brittle, fragrant peppers.

Peperoni cruschi are more than a mere snack. They occupy a sizeable place in the Lucanian kitchen. They were introduced to the area by the Spanish rulers in the seventeenth century and flourished in the warm air of the Sini valley. Easy to grow, easy to dry, easy to transport, easy to store, they quickly found a warm welcome in kitchens throughout the region. The carmine red horn-shaped peppers are picked in August, then strung on long strings to dry. These are called *'serte'*, and if you keep a look out you will spot vertical stripes of red hanging from balconies, in greengrocers or delicatessens, on restaurant walls as you stroll through the streets of Senise and towns and villages across Basilicata.

Locally they are often referred to as *zafaran*, particularly when ground to a powder. Wishful thinking – it does look similar to ground saffron but can't command the same high price. Much as you'd expect, it is way closer to a mild (*dulce*) Spanish paprika. So that makes it a much more democratic spice, the kind of thing that every household can afford. The kind of thing that has embedded itself in the heart of Basilicata's culinary repertoire.

Far more than a crisp alternative, they gift their bright colour and sweetness to *soppressata*, a renowned local salami, they turn up on or in stews, with fried *baccalà*, on pasta, on pizzas and way more. In one shop in Senise they even sell them dipped in chocolate. Possibly a step too far, but I admire their enthusiasm.

Manzo alla Maniera della Moglie del Macellaio

Pot Roast Beef with Dried Red Peppers and Pancetta

After a chilly night-time stroll around Senise's atmospheric old town, complete with swirling mists, dark alleys and a startling Christmas display of lights in the form of a wild boar, I warmed up in the busy Manieri family's butcher and deli. As I paid for my skein of dried peppers, the butcher's wife told me how she used them in stews, rehydrated and added at the last minute so that they don't dissolve over long slow cooking.

Such a good tip. This is my interpretation of that brief chat over the clink of coins. It is the perfect wintery pot-roast, with those deep rich flavours that come from slow cooking and the final addition of sweet, supple, rehydrated peppers. In the likely event that you can't get *peperoni cruschi* in a shop near you, mild Mexican *ancho* chillies are a good substitute.

Like most slow-cooked meat dishes, this one tastes even better if made a day in advance, then reheated thoroughly (add an extra few splashes of water), but don't add the rehydrated peppers until you are almost ready to serve.

Serves 4–6

1kg joint braising beef, e.g. chuck or brisket
3 tablespoons extra virgin olive oil
150g pancetta lardons
1 onion, chopped
1 carrot, sliced
1 stem of celery, sliced

4 cloves of garlic, chopped
2 tablespoons chopped parsley
2 bay leaves
1 x 400g tin of chopped tomatoes
salt and freshly ground black pepper
50g dried red *peperoni cruschi* or Mexican *ancho* chillies

Preheat the oven to 150°C/130°C fan/gas 2. Brown the meat in the olive oil in a casserole dish over a high heat. Lift out and set aside. Reduce the heat and add the pancetta, onion, carrot, celery, garlic, parsley and bay leaves to the casserole. Cook gently, until the onion is tender and translucent. Stir in the tinned tomatoes, 200ml of water, salt and freshly ground black pepper. Return the browned beef to the pan. Cover tightly, transfer to the oven and leave to simmer away peacefully for 2–3 hours, until the beef is very tender. Turn the beef every 40 minutes or so.

About 40 minutes before serving, put the peppers into a bowl and cover with boiling water. Leave to soak for 25–30 minutes. Drain, tug out the stems and seeds, then cut the peppers into thirds if they are *peperoni cruschi*, quarters for *anchos*. Stir into the casserole. Cover again and cook for a final 5–10 minutes.

To serve, lift the beef out on to a chopping board and slice thickly with a very sharp knife. Return to the sauce and serve immediately, with polenta, mashed potato or just good bread to wipe the plates clean.

Pasta alla Mollica con Salsiccia e Peperoni Cruschi

Pasta with Breadcrumbs, Sausage and Paprika

Okay, so pasta and breadcrumbs doesn't sound too promising, but when it is done properly the result is delicious, with its mix of soft and crunchy. This version, with sausage as well, is the one they serve at Rotondella's Locando Pane e Lavoro and I urge you to try it. Use lots of ground *peperoni cruschi* or paprika to get the full rounded flavour.

Serves 4

160g best-quality pork sausages
140g dried breadcrumbs
2 cloves of garlic, peeled
350g long macaroni, or spaghetti
3–4 tablespoons extra virgin olive oil
1 heaped teaspoon fennel seeds, roughly crushed
salt and freshly ground black pepper
3 tablespoons ground *peperoni cruschi*, or mild paprika

Put a large pan of water on to boil. Season it generously with salt.

Slit open the skin of the sausages and peel it off. Crumble the sausage meat into small pieces. Whizz the breadcrumbs with the garlic in a food processor.

Once the water is at a rolling boil, add the pasta, give it a good stir and leave to boil until cooked al dente. Meanwhile, heat up a wide frying pan. Add the olive oil and the crumbled sausage meat. Sizzle vigorously for a couple of minutes, until beginning to colour here and there. Now add the garlic bread-crumbs and the crushed fennel. Stir the crumbs and sausage together, keeping it all moving nicely, until the crumbs are golden brown. Season with salt and freshly ground black pepper, then stir in the ground *peperoni cruschi*/paprika. Take off the heat immediately (paprika burns very quickly). Scoop out about a third of the mixture and set aside.

Scoop out a mugful of the pasta water. Drain the pasta. Return the frying pan to the heat, adding about half the reserved pasta water. Stir to make a rough sauce (you may need to add a little more pasta water), then tip in the pasta. Toss it all together, adding a final slurp of pasta water if it seems a little dry. Serve straight away, topping each plateful with a sprinkling of the reserved crisp crumb mixture.

A Hot Tip from a Cool Vet

One afternoon I fell into chatting with the man at the next-door table. He was a vet, keen to practise his English, which was very good. He came from Matera, 2019 European City of Culture, second city in Basilicata, famous and once infamous for its Sassi cave dwellings, catapulted on to the world's screens in James Bond's *No Time to Die*. We spoke a little of cattle and horses and sheep, then inevitably we arrived at food. He told me authoritatively that the best place to eat Matera's *pignata di pecora*, lamb stew, was at a restaurant called the Casino del Diavolo on the edge of the city. Covid intervened, but two years later, I hesitantly followed Google maps' instructions to turn down the untarred lane leading to the surprisingly large, surprisingly full car park of the Devil's Disaster Restaurant.

It is the kind of place that travelling foodies fantasise about. Off the beaten track, packed with Italian families, undiscovered by other foreigners, serving real, local, unprettified dishes with warm confidence and enthusiasm. Within minutes I spotted my first, magnificent *pignata di pecora* emerging from the wood-fired oven. The earthenware dish is sealed tightly with a canopy of dough, burnt and rugged from the heat, and oh good heavens, it's coming my way.

Theatrically, the waiter chipped the crust away, steam hovered and rose in a savoury cloud, revealing a curl of dark greens nestled among potatoes, vegetables and butter-soft lamb. It lived up to my long-gone vet's promise, with the kind of taste that comes only from hours of gentle cooking.

Matera's Pignata di Pecora

Lamb, Potato and Vegetable Casserole

This *pignata* is southern cousin to dishes like Irish stew and Lancashire hot pot, a big pot of filling vegetables flavoured with cheap cuts of meat, left to stew slowly in the embers of the fire (or your oven or slowcooker) until the workers returned exhausted and hungry. Little touches, like a handful of tomatoes, a bunch of wild *cicoria* (chicory), thumbnail slips of sheep's milk cheese, anchor it in the poverty-stricken kitchens of Basilicata. This is the most unsophisticated of recipes, ingredients piled in willy-nilly, but by golly it's good.

Which Bit of the Beast

For an ultra-slow-cooking dish like this you have to buy the meat from a butcher. Supermarkets just sell the more expensive quick-cooking cuts, but what you need are the budget bits: scrag and middle neck, and they have to be on the bone so that you get the maximum flavour out of them. Ask your extremely helpful butcher to chop them into pieces about 4cm thick and more-or-less 10cm long. Rough and ready is fine. Mutton will give a fuller flavour if you can find it, but the scrag of lamb does a fine job too.

The *Pignata* and the Sealing Crust

The *pignata* is the southern Italian casserole dish. Made of earthenware, it looks like a pot-bellied jug with no pouring lip and two handles. It comes with a lid which inevitably gets broken. In pre-foil days, the best replacement was a simple sheet of flour and water dough, laid over the opening and pressed to the sides to seal the *pignata* tightly. It has the added advantage of sealing in flavour and preventing drying out over long hours of cooking. It turns out that this is way more effective than foil and worth using even if there is a lid to the casserole you cook your lamb stew in. Wrapped around the edges, it creates a hermetically sealed pot which requires absolutely no human intervention until the moment it finally comes out of the oven.

Serves 4

500g lamb or mutton on the bone (see opposite)
250g potatoes, peeled and cut into 5cm chunks
1 large onion, cut into thin wedges
200g large cherry tomatoes, halved
2 stems of celery, sliced lengthways, then cut into 10cm
    lengths
2 carrots, thickly sliced
60g pecorino cheese, broken into small knobs
100g pancetta lardons, smoked if you can get them
salt and freshly ground black pepper
150g wild *cicoria* or Swiss chard, cut roughly into 10cm
    pieces

For the sealing crust
200g plain flour

Preheat the oven to 150°C/130°C fan/gas 2. Layer the ingredients, excluding the chard, in a casserole dish, seasoning as you go. Lay the chard on top. Pour in 200ml of water. Cover with a close-fitting lid.

For the sealing crust, mix the flour with enough water to make a soft dough – some 100–130ml. Divide into 4 portions. One at a time, roll each one into a thick sausage, then press it along the edge of the casserole and lid, effectively plastering the lid in place. Repeat with the remaining dough, making sure that there are no gaps for steam to escape. Put the casserole into the oven and leave it completely alone to do its thing for 3 hours for lamb, 4 hours for mutton.

Just before serving, chip off the sealing crust (it comes away fairly cleanly), take off the lid and breathe in the beautiful aroma. Taste and adjust the seasoning, then serve hot and steaming. Make sure everyone has a spoon so that none of the broth is wasted. Pass round good bread to mop up the last of it.

The Witches' Potion

No doubt there are many people who love to sip a small snifter of Liquore Strega at the end of a meal, but I am not one of them. As a drink it gets a total thumbs-down from me. Too sticky, too cloying, too sweet, too medicinal. But wait! A strange thing happens when it is added to cakes or puddings. It is magically transformed into a flavouring of excellence, spreading a delicate aromatic scent throughout. There is surely some strange alchemy at work here. Well, of course there is, for Strega comes from the town of Benevento, the epicentre of legendary witchcraft.

The Strega bottle is a handsome affair. A glass starburst is set slap bang in the middle, at its core a drawing of the impressive 'Stabilimento G. Alberti, Presso La Stazione Ferroviaria': The Establishment of G. Alberti, Next to the Railway Station. Strega has been made in these same premises since 1860. The Alberti family were no fools – they knew that a strong, modern distribution network was essential to success, and what better than the relatively new railway service to take their liqueur out into what was shortly to become the fully unified nation of Italy.

The label below the starburst is intriguing. Semi-framed by the red L of the word 'Liquore' is a wrinkled crone, shawl over her head, broom over her shoulder, familiar owl at her side. Under the 'L', three scantily clad young women dance hand in hand with a pair of devils around the trunk of a tree.

This is the infamous walnut tree of Benevento, growing lusty and proud, the focus of Italy's witches, both local and far flung. They kept their incantations and formulas secret, all except one. This was the spell that would bring any witch flying through the skies to the unhallowed walnut tree.

'Nguento, 'nguento,
mànname a lu nocio 'e Beneviento,
sopra'a ll'acqua e sopra ô viento,
sopra â ogne maletiempo.

Unguent, unguent,
send me to the walnut tree of Benevento,
over the water and over the wind,
over all the stormy weather.

Far away down south, in the little town of Bisignano in Calabria, the local wise women were no longer in the first flush of youth, but they still looked forward to their annual away-night in Benevento. As a stormy midnight tolled, they rubbed their oily unguent on their bodies and began to chant. 'Take me to the walnut tree of Benevento, *under* the water, *under* the wind, *under* the storm clouds.' So upside down and wrong! The wild winds tossed the poor women up into the skies, over the mountains, over Naples, tumbling them down at long last on top of the walnut tree, where their clothes snagged on the branches and they dangled head down, dolefully watching their younger sisters frolicking the night away down below them.

Strega is the Italian for witch, which explains the name and magic of the liqueur. It is viscous and potent (at 40% ABV it's on a par with vodka), stained yellow with saffron, one of the seventy or so botanicals that give it its aromatic thwack. It is not so common outside of Italy and honestly, I wouldn't suggest that you go out of your way to track it down. Replace it with some other syrupy herbal concoction that is lurking at the back of your cupboards – Yellow Chartreuse or Drambuie, for instance, would cast their own perfectly tasty spell on many an Italian dessert.

Calzone di Ricotta

Ricotta, Chocolate and Candied Peel Pie

Ricotta is the unsung, unassuming hero of Italian cooking. Practically every region in Italy lays claim to a gorgeous ricotta-based tart or pie of some sort, and Basilicata is no exception. This *'calzone'* is a double-crusted pie, wrapped around a felicitous mix of sweetened ricotta, chocolate and candied peel. Go all-out Italian and serve it for breakfast on Sunday morning, washed down with a vigorous shot of espresso, or keep it instead for teatime or pudding. Wherever, whenever, it goes well with strawberries and raspberries on the side.

Serves 8

For the pastry
360g plain flour, plus a little extra for rolling out
120g caster sugar
a pinch of salt
180g unsalted butter, chilled and diced
2 eggs
½ teaspoon vanilla extract

For the filling
500g ricotta
2 egg yolks
100g caster sugar
1 tablespoon Strega or some other sweet, herby liqueur,
    e.g. Yellow Chartreuse or even Drambuie
100g candied peel
100g dark chocolate, chopped

To finish
1 egg white, lightly beaten
1½ tablespoons caster sugar

Begin by making the pastry. Put the flour, sugar and salt into a roomy bowl. Add the butter and rub in until you have what looks like a bowl of breadcrumbs. Add the eggs and the vanilla and work together to form a soft dough. You may need to add a tablespoon or so of water. Knead briefly, then divide in two. Roll each piece into a ball, flatten to form a thick disc, then wrap in clingfilm and chill for half an hour.

Preheat the oven to 180°C/160°C fan/gas 4. To make the filling, beat the ricotta with the egg yolks, sugar and Strega. Stir in the candied peel and chocolate. Base-line a 23cm springform cake tin, or tart tin with removable base, with baking parchment.

Roll the first ball of pastry out to a thickness of about 3mm on a lightly floured work surface. Line the tin with the pastry. Fill with the ricotta mixture. Smooth down evenly. Roll out the second ball of pastry and lay over the ricotta mixture. Press the edges together to seal, then trim off the excess pastry. Brush the top with the egg white, then dredge with the caster sugar. Bake for 45 minutes, until golden brown. Eat warm or at room temperature.

Sweet Blessings

Traditional southern Italian *dolce* are almost inevitably connected to the high days of the church year, in other words, to Christmas and Easter and to saints' days. Notable exceptions are *gelati*, ice creams and *tiramisù*, now fully acclimatised into local restaurant menus. Universal refrigeration has made both possible in Italy's hot summers. What a blessing this is, even for someone like me who is not a keen devourer of ice cream. Don't get me wrong, I enjoy a few spoonfuls of ice cream when they come my way, but I don't yearn for a cone the minute the mercury rises. No, what I love are the ice cream- or sorbet-based drinks that you can order in bars.

Current favourites in my neighbourhood are Caffe Centrale's iced tea with lemon *granita*, the corner bar's beer poured over lemon *granita* (loosely akin to a shandy slushy) and lemon *granita* topped up with tonic water. Bit of a theme there. Away from the lemon *granita*, there's also espresso coffee poured over a scoop of vanilla ice cream or better still a scoop of hazelnut ice cream, or creamy coffee *granita* lengthened with soda water. Mmmm, mmm, mmm.

Affordable ice cream is a relatively modern phenomenon. Head back to pre-refrigeration days and it was solely the privilege of the rich. One thing that has surprised me is the number of ancient *neviere*, icehouses, that are scattered throughout the south of Italy. My friend and local explorer, Vito Amico, has discovered at least seven in and near my town of Ceglie Messapica. A quick online search reveals a measles rash of *neviere* right across the region, through Basilicata and Calabria. Sicily, too, is full of them. *Neviere* were deep pits dug down into the ground, then lined with stone and capped with a vaulted stone roof. In the depths of winter, the base and sides were insulated with wadges of straw, then the snow packed firmly inside in deep, compacted layers that turned into hard ice. More straw and earth covered the ice, keeping it cold right through the summer months. There was, apparently, much more winter snow in the south of Italy in those days than there is now. More would be carted down from the mountains of Basilicata and Calabria.

This ingeniously preserved ice was of enormous value in the hot months, particularly in areas where water was scarce. It was used medically to cool fevered patients, and in food production for those who could pay for the luxury. The earliest forms of *granita* were mixtures of shaved ice and flavoured syrups, really very similar to the modern lemon *granita* that I love so much when doused in tea or beer or tonic water.

Disappointingly, my own saints' days have yielded little in the way of edible blessings so far. You'll note the plural 'days': according to Wikipedia there are no less than eight different Santa Sofias to choose from, each with their own special day. The most celebrated of these was a second-century Christian woman living in Rome. She had three daughters, Faith, Hope and Charity. At the behest of Emperor Hadrian, she was ordered to renounce her faith. She wouldn't, not even to save her young daughters, who were consequently tortured and beheaded in front of her. A grim story, but that is the nature of sainthood.

Calzoncelli di Castagne

Chestnut and Chocolate Fritters

I've loved the combination of chocolate and chestnut since forever, so I can't tell you how delighted I was to find them sandwiched together inside a sweet fried *raviolo*. Plumply inviting, ridiculously sweet and rich, *calzoncelli* are traditionally a Christmas treat.

Serves 4–6

extra virgin olive oil and/or sunflower oil, to fry
icing sugar

For the pastry
200g plain flour, plus extra for rolling out
25g caster sugar
a good pinch of salt
1 egg yolk, lightly beaten
50ml extra virgin olive oil
50ml dry white wine

For the filling
50g dark chocolate, chopped
125g sweetened chestnut purée
finely grated zest of ½ an orange
¼ teaspoon ground cinnamon
a pinch of ground cloves
1 egg yolk

First make the pastry. Put the flour into a bowl with the sugar and salt. Make a well in the centre and add the egg yolk, olive oil and wine. Mix to form a soft dough. Form into a ball, wrap in a beeswax cloth or clingfilm and chill for half an hour.

For the filling, set the chocolate, in a bowl, over a pan of gently simmering water, making sure that the base does not come into contact with the water. Leave for a minute, then turn off the heat below. Stir occasionally, until the chocolate is completely melted. Cool until tepid, then mix in the chestnut purée, orange zest, spices and egg yolk.

Line a tray with baking parchment. Divide the pastry in two. Keep one ball wrapped to prevent drying out. Roll the other out thinly, about 2–3mm, on a lightly floured work surface. Stamp out 7cm circles with a biscuit cutter or small glass. Arrange half the circles on the tray. Put a generous teaspoon of the filling in the centre of each circle. Brush the edges lightly with water, then cover each one with a second circle of pastry. Seal the edges firmly. Press all round the edges with the tines of a fork. Repeat with the remaining dough. Gather up the scraps, roll out again and stamp out more circles, then fill as before.

Shortly before serving, heat a ½cm depth of oil in a frying pan. I use a mix of sunflower and olive oil. Fry the pastries until golden brown on each side. Drain briefly on a plate lined with a double layer of kitchen paper. Serve hot, dusted with a little icing sugar.

Picciddat Lucano

Sweet Yeast Bread

This is Basilicata's Easter bread, scented with a waft of lemon zest. It's light and tender and delicious. *Picciddat* is really a domestic country cousin of the more famous *colomba*, the classic Italian Easter cake in the shape of a dove, or a French brioche. As befits a traditional Easter treat, it is enriched with lots of eggs – with the lengthening, warmer days, chickens get into their egg-laying stride after the scarcity of the winter months. If you want to be properly celebratory you can tuck more eggs, whole and in their shells, among the curves of the risen dough before it goes into the oven. Looks cute, very traditional, but personally, I'm happy to forgo hard-baked, shell-on egg on my cake.

In an entirely un-Italian way, I like it best lightly toasted and slathered in salted butter. Just saying . . .

Makes 1 loaf

550g strong white bread flour, plus a little extra for
    dusting tray
100g caster sugar
½ teaspoon salt
finely grated zest of 1 lemon
50ml full cream milk
15g fresh yeast or 1 × 7g sachet of dried yeast
50g lard or butter, at room temperature
4 medium eggs
50ml dry white wine

To glaze
1 egg yolk
1 tablespoon milk

Mix the flour, sugar, salt and lemon zest in a roomy bowl. Make a well in the centre. Warm the milk a little – it should be tepid and no more than that. Crumble in the yeast and stir to dissolve. Put the lard into the well, pour over the yeasty milk, then break in the eggs and add the wine. Mix to form a soft dough. Knead with enthusiasm for 10 minutes, dusting with a little extra flour if absolutely necessary, until smooth and elastic. Return to the bowl, slide into a roomy plastic bag if you have one, or cover with a beeswax cloth or with clingfilm. Leave to rise in a warm place until doubled in volume. This can take 2 or 3 hours, so be patient.

Dust a baking tray with flour. Knead the dough again for a few minutes, then divide into two. Roll each piece out to form a fat sausage roughly 45–50cm long. Twist together loosely, pinching the ends together. Curl the twist round to form a plump, round loaf. Tuck the edges underneath. Lift on to the floured baking tray, cover again and leave to rise in a warm place until double its original size.

Preheat the oven to 180°C/160°C fan/gas 4. Whisk the egg yolk with the milk for the glaze. Brush lightly over the surface of the risen loaf. Bake for 30–35 minutes, until richly browned and glossy. You may need to cover the surface loosely with a sheet of foil towards the end to prevent burning. Tap the underneath of the loaf – if it sounds hollow, your *picciddat* is done. Cool on a wire rack, and enjoy.

Strazzata di Avigliano

Peppery Sandwich Bread

The small hilltop town of Avigliano is like dozens of others, nice enough but hardly exceptional. It bustles in summer and is tombstone quiet in the winter. Like many small towns, however, a little scratching at the surface reveals unsuspected gems. Google *'Avigliano coltelli'* (knives) and up pops a list of three local knifesmiths, alongside images of exquisite slender pocket knives. The *balestra* of Avigliano is a knife with a long history. Traditionally, they were given to women as betrothal pledges, to protect themselves should village lotharios or brigands from the hills threaten their purity. The word *'balestra'* usually translates as a hefty crossbow, but these are elegant, ornate and sharp folding daggers. The olive-leaf slender blades are etched with swirling patterns, the handles inlaid with threads of brass, silver or gold.

Second in line is the way more humble *strazzata*, Avigliano's hoop of a bread seasoned energetically with finely ground black pepper. It had never occurred to me to add pepper to bread dough, so this has come as something of a revelation. The heat barely registers at the first mouthful, building gracefully, tickling the palate a little more with each bite. *Strazzata* is a sandwich bread par excellence. This is totally, wonderfully its life-calling. Cut a big chunk, halve it and stuff it as they do in Avigliano, with slices of ham and cheese, adding perhaps a sliver or two of tomato and some shreds of lettuce. You'd be hard put to get a better sandwich.

Makes 1 loaf

250g semolina flour or strong white or wholemeal bread
    flour, plus a little extra for kneading and baking
250g 00 flour
10g salt
7–8g freshly ground black pepper
around 350ml warm water
15g fresh yeast or 1 × 7g sachet of dried yeast
a little extra virgin olive oil

Mix the two flours, salt and freshly ground black pepper together. Make a well in the centre and add a generous slurp of the warm water. Crumble in the fresh yeast or tip in the dried. With your fingers, cream the yeast in the water, gradually bring- ing in some of the flour. Add the rest of the water a little at a time, mixing well, to form a soft dough.

Knead the dough on a lightly floured work surface for a good 10 minutes or so, until smooth (apart from the odd knobble of pepper) and very elastic. Form into a ball. Drizzle a little olive oil into the mixing bowl and turn the ball of dough in the oil so that it is lightly coated. Cover with clingfilm or slide into a roomy plastic bag and tuck the ends underneath. Leave for 1–2 hours in a warm place, until doubled in bulk.

Sprinkle a baking tray with flour. Scoop the bread dough out of the bowl and knead for a few minutes to smooth out. Form into a ball again, then flatten out to a disc some 2–3cm thick. Place on the baking tray. With your fingers, make a hole in the centre, then work the dough out gently to form a ring. When it is done, the central hole should measure roughly 12–13cm in diameter. Sprinkle a little more flour on top, then cover loosely with clingfilm or slide into a roomy plastic bag. Leave to rise for another 30–60 minutes in a warm place, until proudly puffed.

Preheat the oven to 220°C/200°C fan/gas 7. Uncover the ring of dough and bake for 25 minutes, until golden brown. Cool on a wire rack.

Strazzato al Oregano e Pancetta

Strazzato with Oregano and Pancetta

As opposite, but knead 1½ tablespoons of dried oregano and 120g of pancetta, diced and fried in its own fat, into the dough after the first rise.

This makes it more of a stand-alone bread, the kind that a foreigner, like me, would like to dip into a little bowl of olive oil with a few drops of balsamic vinegar floating around in it, while waiting for the first course to arrive. This is so not Italian, but damn it, it tastes good.

Calabria

Travelling in the Broth of Nostalgia

In 1967, the travel writer H. V. Morton took a long, curious trip around the Mezzogiorno, snaking his way from the Abruzzo down through Puglia, to Basilicata, Naples and finally back down to Calabria. His book *A Traveller in Southern Italy* was my companion fifteen years later when I first fell for Italy's southernmost extremes. Following his trail, I took the train from Reggio Calabria south along the coast, then the juddering bus up into the foothills of the Aspromonte to the small town of Stilo.

There was only one hotel, an impossibly romantic old *palazzo*. The owners spent their day in the relative cool of the arched entrance hall, playing cards and gossiping. Upstairs the corridor led past beautiful dusty reception rooms, red velvet curtains drawn against the August heat. Next morning their son gave me a handful of wrinkled red fruits, not much bigger than olives, from a tree in the lush, shady garden. Jujubes, or *giuggiole* in Italian. Sweet, a little fudgy, not a remarkable fruit but good enough to ease the steep, hot climb up out of the village to La Cattolica, Stilo's precious claim to fame. Though not common, jujubes are familiar enough to have generated the peculiar expression '*andare in brodo di giuggiole*', 'to go in jujube broth'. It means being in a state of supreme contentment, which by coincidence is pretty much where I was that day.

Not so much the following morning, mind you, when I was all but arrested by the local *carabinieri* while waiting for the bus back down to the coast. My crime was to be young, alone, female and foreign on a day when the police had nothing better to occupy their time. Two slow, anxious hours later, the bus long gone, they released me from the confines of the police station.

As I strolled down towards the old town a few weeks ago, I noticed that police station is still there, sheltered by the grand façade of the Chiesa di San Giovanni Therestis. Meanwhile, the *palazzo*, once lovely Hotel San Giorgio, is boarded up and long abandoned. Nostalgically, I wished that it might have been the other way round. This time I drove up to La Cattolica, the pretty little Byzantine church that sports a reputation far greater than its petite but perfect floor plan.

I'm brave enough now to admit that I found it a tad disappointing, both all those years ago and this time round. The location, on the other hand, is just as blessed, with views across to the blue sea, Stilo perched below, and even better, next to the fabulous Chiosco Bar. This fine café in a wooden hut is the creation of Tonino, who also claims to have created the first and best bergamot ice cream. He may well be right on both counts.

Once upon a time you might have been able to pick out the many bergamot orchards in the valley below La Cattolica. Bergamots were big, big business. The fruit, about the size of a large orange, is thought to be a cross between a lemon and a bitter orange. They were grown for the perfumed oil in their skins, an essential component in the perfumery industry and the flavour of Earl Grey tea.

Bergamot's past glory was based not only on its heady perfume but also on its capacity to anchor scent on the skin, ensuring that it lingers seductively wherever it is dabbed. It was a major component of the original and much imitated Eau de Cologne, created by the Farina company in the early eighteenth century in Cologne. Their roster of notable customers includes Beethoven, Oscar Wilde and Queen Victoria. Back in the bergamot orchards in Calabria, the workers painstakingly sponged the oils from the fruit, squeezing the precious drops into vials for transportation. Quite how Earl Grey tea earned its moniker is a bit of a mystery. Sure, Earl Grey himself was

Queen Victoria's prime minister for four years, 1830–34, but curiously the first printed reference to Earl Grey tea turns up way after he died. There is a very plausible suggestion that the bergamot oil was actually blended with second-rate tea to disguise its shortcomings. The rebranding of this bottom-of-the-tea-chest cheapo beverage as Earl Grey tea was a genius marketing ploy, gifting an aspirational grandeur to it.

The bergamot tree is picky about where it grows. This sweep of the Calabrian coast, from Scilla down round Italy's toe and up the south-eastern Calabrian coast, is where it is happiest and most productive. For centuries it was such a major cash cow for orchard owners that they told their workers that the juice of the fruit was poisonous, in a bid to prevent pilfering. This turns out to be totally untrue. It's delicious. The conference room of the fascinating Museo del Bergamotto in Reggio Calabria is hung with photos of a host of Italian notables, including many TV personalities from the '90s. These are the archives of another marketing campaign attempting to persuade Calabrians that *spremuta di bergamotto*, freshly squeezed bergamot juice, is not merely safe to drink, but positively life-enhancing.

The twentieth century had seen the development of cheap synthetic alternatives to bergamot oil, a death knell for so many of the Calabrian orchards. Enthusiasts have been fighting to save the last of them. Nowadays there's something of a small revival, thanks to local entrepreneurs making bergamot soaps and lotions, bottling the juice, boiling up jams and jellies and freezing *gelati* and *granite* in Tonino's wake.

In the autumn, I buy green-skinned bergamots from my local supermarket and greengrocer in Puglia. At this stage, the essential oil is at its best and most prolific. This is the time to candy their peel, ready for Christmas cooking, or to make your own *bergamino*, bergamot liqueur. The juice is almost as sharp as lemon juice, so use it in salad dressings or marinades.

As the winter sets in, the fruits ripen to a lemony yellow. The heady perfume of the oil diminishes a little, and the juice becomes more plentiful and less acidic. By January, they are ready for marmalade or a bergamot curd. The grated zest will still be fragrant enough for cakes and baking (bergamot drizzle cake is divine), or just drink the juice, diluted with water and sweetened to taste. Whichever way, it's a win-win situation for a cook and her company.

Marmellata di Bergamotte all'Inglese with Optional Limoncello

Bergamot and Lemon Marmalade

Bergamots make the best marmalade ever. This is a recipe for a British-style marmalade with long shreds of tender peel, not the Italian *marmellata* with its semi-puréed consistency. Sometimes I stir in a few shots of limoncello for extra zip, but to be honest I still can't decide whether I prefer it with or without.

Makes 8–10 jars

around 1kg bergamots (4 large ones)
2 large lemons
2.5kg granulated sugar
4–6 tablespoons limoncello (optional)

Day 1: Cut the bergamots and lemons in half and squeeze the juice out of all of them. Tip it into a large bowl. Line another medium-sized mixing bowl with a large square of muslin or a clean tea towel. Scrape out as much of the pulp left in the fruit shells as you can into the lined bowl. Begin with a dessertspoon, then use your fingers to tug the loose flaps away until you are left with more-or-less pristine shells. Put all the scrappy bits into the lined bowl. Gather up the edges of the cloth and tie together firmly with string to form a pouch. With a sharp knife, quarter the bergamot and lemon shells, cutting out and discarding the tough green stem bases. Cut the quarters into fine shreds. Put these into the bowl of juice, then add the pouch of debris and 3 litres of water. Cover and leave to stand overnight.

Day 2: Tip the whole lot into a large preserving pan. Bring up to the boil and simmer for around 1 hour, until the strips of peel are very tender. Let it cool for half an hour or so, then lift out the bag and squeeze hard to extract the last of the pectin-rich juice into the pan. Now you can bin the contents of the bag.

While the pan is simmering, put two or three saucers into the freezer. Sterilise your jam jars (see page 108), leaving them in the oven to keep warm.

Add the sugar to the preserving pan of juice. Put the pan over a moderate heat and stir until the sugar has completely dissolved, without letting it boil. Bring up to the boil and boil hard for about 10 minutes. Turn off the heat and drip a few drops on to one of the chilled saucers. Let it sit for 3 or 4 minutes, then nudge with your fingernail. If the surface wrinkles, your marmalade is ready. If not, turn the heat back on under the pan and boil for another 5 minutes. Repeat until setting point is reached.

Let the marmalade cool for half an hour (so that it thickens enough to prevent the bergamot shreds from floating to the top of the jars), stir in the limoncello if using, then ladle into the hot sterilised jars and seal tightly. Turn the jars upside down and leave for a couple of minutes, then turn them back the right way up, label and store in a cool, dark cupboard until you are ready to dip in. Once opened, store in the fridge.

Bergamino

Bergamot Liqueur

Bergamino is the Calabrian equivalent of limoncello, a sweet potent liqueur to sip at the end of a meal ostensibly to help your digestion. As you would expect from something made with bergamots, it is more scented, but every bit as good when sipped straight from the freezer on a warm summer night.

Makes about 1 litre

4 bergamots (or 6 lemons)
400ml 96% proof alcohol or vodka
350g caster sugar

Peel the green/yellow zest off the bergamots with a vegetable peeler, bringing with it as little of the bitter white pith as possible. Drop the zest into a bowl and pour in the alcohol. Cover tightly with clingfilm and leave in a dark cupboard (not the fridge) for 2 weeks, stirring once a day.

If you are using 96% proof alcohol, put 700ml of water into a saucepan together with the sugar. Stir over a moderate heat until the sugar has completely dissolved, bring up to the boil, then take off the heat and leave to cool. If you are using vodka, use just 500ml of water.

Strain the bergamot-scented alcohol through a muslin-lined sieve and discard the exhausted shreds of peel. Mix the alcohol with the syrup, bottle and leave to settle for one more week before drinking.

Waste Management

Today there is a van on the corner of the street, tail gate down, displaying a wall of fresh purple silver artichokes at a bargain price of ten for 2 euros. The salesman is checking out his phone, tapping the ash nonchalantly from another fag, waiting for customers or a mate to gossip with. This is a sure sign that the artichoke season is at its height but that they won't be around for much longer. They're the small, everyday artichokes that come in leafy bunches, not the hefty, blousy globes that are more common in the north of Europe. Preparing them for cooking is a labour of love, or at least of monumental patience. My downstairs neighbour Maria practically disappears behind the mound of untrimmed artichokes on one side of the table and the mound of trimmings on the other when she is laying up her jars of preserved *carciofi sott'olio* for the summer months.

Like Maria, I usually pile the voluminous discard straight into the food waste caddy. Gardeners tell me the tough fibrous leaves are a fine addition to the compost heap, but there's no room and no need for that on my balcony. I once threw a pile of artichoke scraps into a pot of simmering stock. It was a big mistake. The stock was so bitter I poured it straight down the sink. One friend boils the leaves for an hour or two, then squidges them through a food mill to extract an intense artichoke purée for flavouring a risotto or pasta or to stir, sparingly, into mayonnaise. I admire the concept but I'm not convinced that it is worth the extra faff.

By far and away the most inspired repurposing scheme was that of brothers Angelo, Amedeo and Mario Dalle Molle, back in the late 1940s, round about the time that Italy was heading into its post-war boom years. I'm guessing that they were raised in a family that relished artichokes; three little boys guzzling them down with nary a thought for the hours of kitchen labour behind the delicious mouthfuls. Grown-up Angelo became convinced that there was a way to make money from artichoke debris, and that's precisely what they did. Cynar was launched in 1952 – an intensely bitter *amaro* that makes a fabulous spritz. The Dalle Molle gang ran a magnificent marketing campaign, starting with an iconic red label overlaid with a handsome green artichoke and the slogan 'Contro il logorio della vita moderna'; thwarting the wear and tear of modern life. As waste management schemes go, that's right up my street.

PS: in case you need it, here's the Spritz formula – 3:2:1. In other words, three parts prosecco, two parts Cynar (or Campari or Aperol, in descending order of bitterness), one part sparkling water. Adjust to your taste buds' satisfaction, and serve over ice, garnished with a twist of lemon or orange zest.

Preparing artichoke hearts, big or little

Begin by squeezing the juice of half a lemon into a bowl of cold water and drop the squeezed lemon shell in there too. Working one at a time, slice the stems off an artichoke about 6cm below the main body. Snap off the outer leaves, working your way around and around until you get to the softer inner leaves. Use a vegetable peeler or a small knife to pare off the tough outer layer of the stalk and base. Turn the artichokes on their sides and cut off the upper cone of leaves about 2cm above the base. Quarter the artichokes lengthways and scrape out the hairy choke. In small Italian artichokes there won't be much, but globe artichokes will be more hirsute. Make sure you get rid of every last bit. Return the pieces to the bowl of lemony water.

Carpaccio di Carciofi

Raw Artichoke Salad

This is the simplest of all artichoke recipes but it only works if a) your artichokes are very, very fresh and b) you slice them incredibly thinly. Either serve it as soon as they are sliced and dressed, at which point they will retain their full crispness, or leave to marinate for a few hours or overnight in the fridge to soften before you add the Parmesan and dig in. Serve as part of an *antipasto*, alongside a platter of *prosciutto crudo* and salamis, or with fish.

Serves 4–6 as part of an *antipasto*

1 globe artichoke or 4 small Italian artichokes, trimmed
juice of 1 lemon
leaves of 2 sprigs of mint, roughly chopped
1 tablespoon chopped parsley
4 tablespoons extra virgin olive oil
salt and freshly ground black pepper
30–45g Parmesan shavings

Slice the artichoke paper thin, then toss with all the remaining ingredients except the Parmesan. Just before serving, check and adjust the seasoning and shave the Parmesan over the top.

La Ciaudedda

Calabrian Spring Artichokes with Broad Beans

Ciaudedda is a dish for that short season when cold weather artichokes overlap with the spring's crop of new broad beans. In the south of Italy that falls in March and April, just as the weather is beginning to warm and spring is finally in the air. It is not a dish for cooks in a hurry. You'll need time and patience for preparing artichokes and podding broad beans. It works well with frozen broad beans, but in that case, it really pays to spend time skinning the individual beans, so not much time is saved there.

Though it is a *contorno*, a side dish, it deserves to be in the spotlight, so partner it with something that won't overwhelm – roast chicken, perhaps, or seared fish steaks.

Serves 6 as a side dish

2 globe artichokes or 8 small Italian artichokes, trimmed
4 tablespoons extra virgin olive oil
2 red onions, thickly sliced
150g pancetta lardons
500g potatoes, peeled and cut into 4cm chunks
3 tablespoons chopped parsley
salt and freshly ground black pepper
1kg broad beans in their pods, or 250g podded broad
    beans, defrosted if frozen

If you are using globe artichokes, cut each one into 12 wedges. Quarter small Italian artichokes lengthways. Drop them back into their acidulated water bath while you start cooking the *ciaudedda*.

Put the olive oil, onions and pancetta into a deep, roomy sauté pan or saucepan. Set over a moderate heat and stir. Let the mixture cook for 5–10 minutes, stirring occasionally, until the onions are floppy. Drain the artichokes and add to the pan, together with the potatoes and the chopped parsley, salt and freshly ground black pepper. Sweat them all together for a couple of minutes, then pour in 300ml of water. Cover and cook gently for another 10–15 minutes, until the potatoes are tender.

While they are cooking, peel the outer skin carefully off larger broad beans if they are freshly podded. If you are using frozen broad beans, slip them all out of their tough outer skin. Add them to the pan, stir in, and add a splash more water if you think it really needs it to prevent catching on the base. Cover again and cook for a final 3–5 minutes, until the broad beans are just cooked. Taste and adjust the seasoning and serve hot, warm or at room temperature.

Amaro di Foglie di Carciofi

Artichoke Leaf Liqueur

Taking a leaf out of the Dalle Molle brothers' book, this is my home-made equivalent of their more complex Cynar. It doesn't use up a massive amount of artichoke detritus but it's way, way better than nothing. The end result is a rather delightful bitter-sweet *amaro* to sip at the end of a meal – so good for the digestion, according to Italian diners – or as the base for a spritz or other cocktail.

Makes about 1 litre

200g artichoke leaves
thinly pared zest of 1 lemon
500ml grappa or vodka
400g caster sugar

Put the artichoke leaves and lemon zest into a bowl and pour over the grappa or vodka. Stir, then cover with clingfilm and leave, at room temperature, for 2 weeks, stirring occasionally.

When the fortnight has elapsed, put the sugar into a saucepan with 400ml of water. Stir over a high heat until the sugar has completely dissolved. Leave to cool. Line a sieve with muslin (or use coffee filters, cut open) and strain the artichoke leaf/ grappa through it. Discard the solids. Mix the grappa with the sugar syrup and pour into sterilised bottles (see page 108). Seal and leave somewhere out of the way for at least another week, preferably 2 or 3, before sipping at your first snifter.

Pipi e Patati

Fried Peppers and Potatoes

An almost ubiquitous Calabrian *contorno* (side dish), with its dialect name that none but the most po-faced English speaker can help but giggle at. It goes with practically anything – a fried or poached egg or two, fennel-spiked sausages, roast chicken, a juicy burger – but I'm happy to dig into a bowlful all on its own.

Italian red peppers are big and twisty and nearly always patched with a splash or more of dark green, which brings its own umami flavour to the capsicum sweetness. In lands where peppers are small and evenly coloured, it pays to include a green pepper alongside red or yellow ones to induce a more rounded flavour.

Serves 4

500g potatoes
2 red peppers (or 1 red and 1 yellow)
1 green pepper
5 tablespoons extra virgin olive oil
salt
1 heaped teaspoon dried oregano (optional)

Peel the potatoes and cut them into wedges, no more than 1cm thick at the thickest part. Trim the peppers, deseed and quarter. Then cut into broad strips.

Heat 3 tablespoons of the olive oil in a wide, deep frying pan over a lively heat. Sauté the peppers in the oil until they begin to soften and catch at the edges. Scoop out on to a plate with a slotted spoon, allowing excess oil to fall back into the pan.

Return the pan to the heat and turn it down a little. Add the potatoes and the rest of the oil. Spread the potatoes out so that they overlap as little as possible. Cover with a lid and leave for 4–5 minutes until browned underneath. Turn the pieces over and repeat until the potatoes are very nearly cooked through. Slide the peppers back into the pan and season generously with salt. Add the oregano if using. Now fry for a few more minutes, until the potatoes are soft and the peppers are smoking hot. Taste and adjust the seasoning, then serve.

Zimbato or Ciambotto di Verdure

Red Pepper, Aubergine and Potato Mess

A great big gorgeous vegetable fry-up, that's what this is. Workers' fare across the region, from heel to toe. There are dozens of variations on the theme, adding different vegetables here and there, but essentials are aubergine, peppers, potatoes and tomatoes. Personally, that's all I need, and more to the point, all I can fit into my largest frying pan at one go. Eat it hot, warm (best of all) or at room temperature. Eat it as a main course with nothing more than some decent bread on the side, or as an all-in-one side dish with anything from a couple of poached or fried eggs to a golden roast chicken. Eat it at home, at work or take it on a picnic on a sunny day.

You don't absolutely need to salt the aubergine but it does improve the flavour a tad, so you might as well let it drip its salty tears while you chop the other ingredients. Most Calabrian cooks would, I think, peel the potatoes, but I don't.

Serves 4–6 as a main course, 6 as a side dish

1 large aubergine
salt and freshly ground black pepper
2 red peppers
400g potatoes
4 tablespoons extra virgin olive oil
4 cloves of garlic, chopped
1 red chilli, finely chopped
500g tomatoes, roughly chopped
a good handful of basil leaves

Cut the aubergine into 1½cm thick chips. Spread out in a colander and toss with a good sprinkling of salt. Leave to drain while you prepare the rest of the vegetables.

Deseed the peppers and cut into strips. Cut the potatoes into wedges about 1cm thick at the thickest part.

Put 2 tablespoons of olive oil into a wide frying pan over a high heat. Sauté the peppers until they are half cooked, then scoop out with a slotted spoon, letting excess oil drip back into the frying pan. Pat the aubergine dry with kitchen paper. Fry in the oil remaining in the pan, adding more as needed, until patched with brown. Scoop out and add to the peppers.

Add the last of the oil to the frying pan. Tip in the potato wedges, smooth down into a single flattish layer and leave undisturbed for 2–3 minutes or so, until browned underneath. Turn over and repeat. Add 150ml of water to the pan, clamp on the lid, and reduce the heat. Cook for another 5 minutes, until the potatoes are nearly tender and the water has been absorbed. Return the peppers and aubergine to the pan, add the garlic and chilli and sauté for a minute or so. Finally, stir in the tomatoes and basil, and season generously. Cover again and leave to cook for another 8–10 minutes, stirring once.

Check that the potatoes are totally cooked through. Taste and adjust the seasoning, and serve hot or warm or at room temperature.

Ciambotto in Pane

Ciambotto Picnic Loaf

In those long-ago pre-plastic-lunchbox days, workers still had to find some way of taking their midday meal with them. In Cornwall (or Devon), the Cornish (or Devon) pasty was a neat solution to carrying sustenance to the fields or down the tin mines, while over in Bedfordshire there was the clanger, a suet roll with savoury filling at one end, sweet at the other. Natty idea. In Puglia, Basilicata and Calabria, many agricultural workers' days began before dawn with a long, long walk, from the hilltop town which offered safety and shelter at night, down to the fields and farms in the valleys.

A friend of mine recalls this happening as late as the 1960s, when he was a boy living in my town of Ceglie Messapica. In the early morning, the streets reverberated with the sound of sheep, goats and cattle being herded out of their stables to head off to the pasture for the day. Eight decades on those stables have mostly been transformed into bijou little '*monolocale*', small one-roomed homes with beds in alcoves and an '*angolo cucina*' – starter homes for young couples, finisher homes for the retired and an inevitable multiplicity of Airbnb's for summer visitors.

The sturdy crust of a loaf baked in the wood-fired oven was the obvious solution, not only portable and fillable but also edible, especially when softened from the inside with the juices of tomatoes and vegetables.

It's an idea that is eminently revivable when you are next planning a picnic. The night before, make up a batch of *zimbato* (see page 214) but resist the temptation to eat it there and then. Next morning, take a good sturdy round loaf of bread – a sourdough is ideal, but even a commercial *pain de campagne* style of loaf works well – and carefully cut off the top, angling the knife down and inwards to make a lid that will sit snugly back on to the loaf. Carefully pull out the crumb and set aside for some other dish at some later time. Don't be over-enthusiastic. You want to end up with a bread bowl, a couple of centimetres thick all round. Stir the *zimbato*, then pile it into the loaf, packing it in firmly. Replace the bread lid, pressing it down gently. Wrap in greaseproof paper or foil. If there is time to spare, weight it down for a while to compact filling and bread; I lay a bag of rice or beans on top. It will cut more neatly when the time comes. Remember to pack the bread knife, and cut the loaf into wedges when you are ready to eat.

World Domination Does Not Bring Happiness but 'Nduja Might

The small town of Spilinga is one of the most miserable places I've ever been to. As I drove in, I wondered how many decades ago it had been abandoned. Semi-derelict houses seemed on the verge of collapse, unloved and empty. A crumbling greyness hung over the empty streets. I persevered beyond the outskirts, searching for Spilinga's vibrant heart. Nothing doing. I strode the grey, silent streets for half an hour and left.

Spilinga's sizeable claim to fame is that it is the birthplace of *'nduja*. If you don't know what that is, where have you been for the last decade? *'Nduja* is a beltingly, devilishly chilli-hot spreadable salami, fabulous on pizzas, in sauces, on toast, stirred into tomato sauce or chicken stew. Brilliant stuff. In recent years it has finally made it to the big time, escaping the confines of Calabria, leaping on to menus across the world in all the most fashionable of places. Smugly, I'd like to make it clear that I have known about it since the early 1980s, way before today's smart Alecs of the foodie world.

Smugness aside, I'd nurtured a mini-fantasy of eating *'nduja* at its point of origin. Nothing fancy – just a simple *panino* with a smear of the red stuff inside, a slice or two of mozzarella over that, a few tomatoes or a little rocket if I was lucky. Hell, I'd settle for a d.i.y. bread roll from the baker's, and a knob of *'nduja* from a corner shop, roughly cobbled together in the car, if necessary.

I left Spilinga empty-handed, empty-stomached and mightily puzzled. Where was the pride and joy and prosperity that I had expected? Damn it, where was the *'nduja*? I spotted one lonely sign for it outside a very closed butcher's unit, so, sighing, I escaped to a happier place in the form of a neat little restaurant hidden in a happier town some ten minutes' drive away. The *'nduja* producers, it turns out, cluster in a kind of fiery tourniquet just beyond the limits of Spilinga. If they are reaping the rewards of world dominance, then precious little of it is being spent in the town that begat their trade.

Frittata di 'Nduja e Friggitelli

'Nduja and Green Pepper Frittata

Unsurprisingly, *'nduja* features frequently on the menu at La Casareccia restaurant in nearby Brattiró. The two high points were the *'nduja bruschetta*, flashed under a hot grill, and a wedge of this frittata among the *antipasti*. Make sure the grill is good and hot and get the frying pan as close as possible to frizzle the edges of the *'nduja*.

**Serves 3–4 as a light main course,
6 as part of an *antipasto***

6 eggs
45g freshly grated Parmesan
2 heaped tablespoons finely chopped parsley
1 clove of garlic, crushed
salt and freshly ground black pepper
150g *friggitelli* peppers or 1 green pepper, deseeded and
    thinly sliced
3 tablespoons extra virgin olive oil
45–60g *'nduja*, depending on how big a hit you want

Preheat the grill. Whisk the eggs with the Parmesan, parsley, garlic, a little salt and lots of freshly ground black pepper.

Put the peppers and the olive oil into a 26cm frying pan and place over a medium heat. Fry until the peppers are barely soft. Raise the heat. Stir the egg mixture again, then pour into the pan. Reduce the heat and quickly dot scant teaspoons of the *'nduja* as evenly as you can over the eggs. Let it cook for another 3–4 minutes, until the underneath is browned.

Place the pan under the grill and leave for a few more minutes, until set and patched with brown.

Slide out on to a plate and eat warm or at room temperature.

Zuppa di Borlotti, Bietole, Patate e 'Nduja

Borlotti, Swiss Chard, Potato and 'Nduja Soup

In cold weather Calabrians turn to steamy, thick bean or lentil soups. They are comforting, warming and filling. This soup is spiced with a generous knob of 'nduja and lightened with a last minute handful of leafy chard.

Serves 4–6

350g dried borlotti beans, soaked overnight, or 2 × 400g tins of borlotti beans
3 tablespoons extra virgin olive oil, plus a little extra to serve
1 onion, chopped
1 carrot, diced
1 stem of celery, thinly sliced
3 cloves of garlic, chopped
2 sprigs of thyme
100g passata
2 tablespoons chopped parsley
salt and freshly ground black pepper
200g potatoes, peeled and diced
a handful of basil leaves
200g Swiss chard
35–50g 'nduja

If using dried beans, drain them and put them into a saucepan with water to cover generously and a few pinches of salt. Bring up to the boil, then reduce the heat and simmer until tender.

Drain, reserving the water. If using tinned beans, just drain and rinse them.

Meanwhile, put the olive oil into a saucepan with the onion, carrot, celery, garlic and thyme. Set over a moderately low heat and fry gently until the onion is tender and translucent. Add the passata, parsley, salt, freshly ground black pepper and 100ml of water. Cover and simmer together for about 20 minutes. Now add the beans and enough of their cooking water, or tap water if using tinned, to cover generously. Add the potatoes and basil too. Simmer for another 15–20 minutes, until the potatoes are tender and the liquid is thickening a little.

While that's all simmering away merrily, stack the chard up in a heap on your chopping board, then cut across the leaves into 2cm wide strips. Add them to the pan of soup, and simmer for a final 5 minutes until it is tender. Stir in the 'nduja. Taste, adjust the seasoning and serve.

Petto di Pollo Ripieno di 'Nduja e Ricotta

Chicken Stuffed with 'Nduja and Wrapped in Prosciutto Crudo

I noticed early on in my life here in the south of Italy that it is rare to find a chicken dish on a restaurant menu. That was in Puglia, but the same seems to be true of Basilicata and Calabria. It's not that people don't eat chicken, just that they don't think it merits attention or note, and it certainly doesn't deserve space on a professional menu. Cegliese friends have dismissed chicken as diet food or invalid food, which comes as something of a surprise to a Brit like me who adores chicken with all its magnificent potential.

So, even though this excellent recipe reads like it comes from somewhere down south, what with its charge of cannellini beans, cherry tomatoes, olive oil, ricotta and above all, *'nduja*, it doesn't. It actually comes from a favourite food blog, the witty, intelligent, delicious Nutmegs, Seven (www.nutmegsseven.co.uk) written by Elly McCausland. Thank you, Elly!

Serves 4

2 × 400g tins of cannellini beans, drained and rinsed
2 tablespoons extra virgin olive oil, plus extra for drizzling
2 cloves of garlic, crushed
12 cherry tomatoes, halved
150g baby spinach, plus extra to serve
salt and freshly ground black pepper
1 tablespoon dried oregano

100g ricotta
4 free-range chicken breasts
30g 'nduja
8 slices of prosciutto crudo

Preheat the oven to 180°C/160°C fan/gas 4. In a large baking dish, toss the cannellini beans with the olive oil, garlic, cherry tomatoes, spinach, salt and freshly ground black pepper, and half the oregano.

Mix the rest of the oregano into the ricotta, along with salt and freshly ground black pepper. Slice a chicken breast lengthways, almost in half but not quite, to create a pocket for stuffing. Spread a quarter of the 'nduja into the gap, then a quarter of the ricotta. Place 2 slices of prosciutto crudo next to each other on a chopping board, slightly overlapping, then wrap the chicken in them. Place on top of the cannellini bean and spinach mixture.

Repeat with the remaining chicken breasts, 'nduja, ricotta and ham. Season the wrapped chicken breasts, drizzle with a little more oil, then place in the oven for 40 minutes, or until the chicken is cooked and opaque at its thickest part, and its juices run clear (it's quite hard to tell because of the red 'nduja stuffing, so err on the side of caution). Serve immediately on a bed of more baby spinach.

Camigliatello

Camigliatello is famous throughout the south of Italy for all of the following: potatoes, skiing, good food, mushrooms (more precisely *porcini*, *Boletus edulis*), its height above sea level (1,272 metres), its gateway status for the Parco della Sila, and chestnuts. For a small town it boasts a phenomenal number of hotels, blessed as it is with a double tourist season both mid-winter and midsummer. Its roofs slope in alpine fashion (the area has been called the Italian Switzerland) but to be honest, it is not particularly pretty. And yet, and yet, I can't help but love it.

The broad main street (there aren't that many other streets) slopes uphill, lined with fascinating shops and neat little restaurants. Next to the über-smart kitchenware shop is a *coltelleria*, a knife shop, full of blades for whittling, slashing, chopping, paring. There's a disturbingly garish display in the window of the 'artistic fabric' shop, toddlers' snowboots and hiking gear in the general store. The proprietor of the fabulous Macelleria Sila dei Fratelli Falcone tells me that he took over from his uncle, who died a few years ago. He makes the sausages seasoned with *porcini*, the hams, the salamis, pancetta and *guanciale* that festoon the tiled walls. I buy smoked ricotta, chestnut flour bread rolls and dried *porcini* to take home with me.

The Sila is one of Calabria's three *parchi nazionali*, nature reserves, sandwiched between the Pollino and Aspromonte heights. It comes as something of a surprise to find ski resorts in the very south of Italy, just a spit and a lick from the shores of the Mediterranean sea, but they exist, albeit with a comparatively short season. Camigliatello may not have the cachet of Chamonix or Aspen, but I'd bet my bottom euro that the pasta and the wild boar sausages are better here.

For a few days in the autumn the street is thronged with visitors to the Festa dei Porcini. Giant illuminated mushrooms dangle above an endless vista of crates filled with fresh *porcini* culled from secret spots in the surrounding hills. No wonder we hadn't found a scrap of a mushroom of any sort when we'd been stumbling through steep wooded slopes earlier that morning. As we gaze at yet another abundant display of tawny dried *porcini*, my inner sceptic whispers that they can't possibly all emanate from the immediate vicinity, or even from Calabria. Ssh! Ssh! Don't ruin the spectacle, inner sceptic! The cult of the *Boletus edulis* is alive and strong in Camigli-atello and deserves full ritual devotion and celebration.

By March, when I twist and turn my car up from Cosenza for my second visit, there are still scraps of snow at the edges of the roads. Skiers and fresh *porcini* merchants are gone, but the shoulder-high wooden mushroom is still there to greet visitors as they turn into the via Roma, the main street. There aren't many places open for lunch but at the all-purpose bar-pizzeria-ristorante Giadi the special mushroom menu page lists: *insalata di porcini* (in season only), *porcini grigliati* (grilled) and *porcini impanati e fritti*, breaded fried *porcini*. That's good enough for me. In the corner a merry family foursome dig into massive mounds of tagliatelle with *porcini*. '*È brutto, mio marito! È cosi brutto!*' giggles mamma as she photographs her husband lovingly. 'My husband, he's so ugly!' And he cheerfully forks another tangle of mushroom tagliatelle into his mouth. I settle for the handmade '*fusilli*', languid ringlets of pasta, with sausage from the Macelleria della Sila next door, smoked ricotta and slithery, savoury, earthy shards of *porcini*. Hurrah, my bottom euro is well and truly safe!

Fileja

Home-made Ringlet Pasta

Southern pasta is a simple affair, just flour and water and deft fingers. Ideally you will use yellow semolina flour (*semola rimacinata*). Good Italian delis may sell it, or you can buy it online. Standard pudding semolina is not a good substitute – way too coarse. 00 flour works fine instead – your finished pasta will just be a little softer and paler.

Travelling through Basilicata and Calabria, by far the most common pasta I came across was an elongated form of macaroni, sometimes spiralled like a ringlet, sometimes more tubular. The name varies from one place to another: *maccaruni, ferretti, firzuli, frizzuli, ferricelli, fileja* and undoubtedly many more. The one essential bit of equipment is a *ferro*, a metal spoke. A spoke from a broken umbrella works very nicely, thank you. What? You threw it out? Fine, then use a wooden skewer instead but dust it lightly with flour first.

Italian pasta makers will always work on an unvarnished wooden work surface – smooth but with just enough grip to make shaping easier. A large wooden chopping board or table are the best surfaces to work on.

Serves 4–6

400g semolina flour or 00 flour, plus extra for trays/
 rolling

Tip the flour out in a heap on your work surface. Make a well in the centre with your fingers so that it looks like a volcanic crater. Pour in about 180ml of hot water. With a fork, gradually stir flour from the volcanic walls into the water. Keep going until it looks

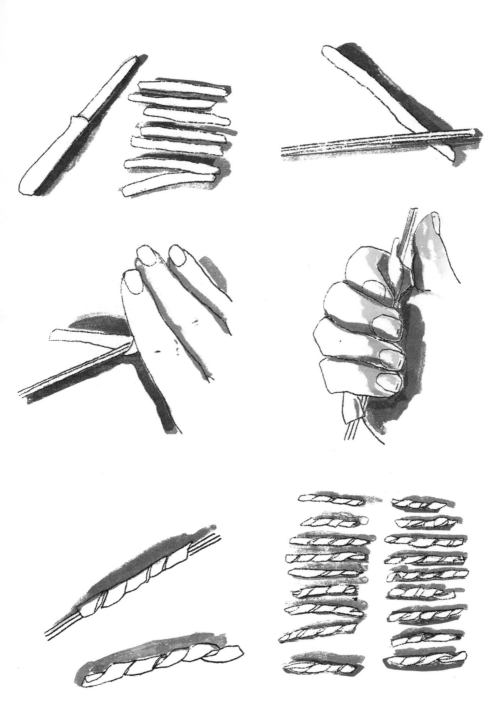

like lumpy scrambled eggs. Flip the remaining flour over the top of the goo, then mix it all together with your fingertips, adding more warm water as needed, until you have a moderately firm dough. Knead the dough for 5 minutes or so until it is smooth and malleable. By now it should be soft enough to shape easily, but firm enough to hold its shape once formed. Roll into a ball and wrap in clingfilm. Leave to rest for at least 20 minutes at room temperature.

Dust two trays or large plates generously with flour. Tear off a walnut-shaped knob of dough. Cover the remainder so that it doesn't dry out. Roll your walnut of dough out to form a long thin pencil-thick sausage. If it is sticking to the work surface, dust the surface and dough lightly with flour. Cut into 8–10cm lengths. Lay the first length of dough diagonally in front of you. Lay your *ferro* or skewer across one end at a 30° angle to the dough. Pressing down lightly, spiral-roll the dough around the *ferro*, so that it flattens as it rolls.

Getting the *fileja* off the rod is the hardest bit. It may require a little practice but I promise, it is not impossible. Hold the rod at one end and lay the bit with the pasta on it in the palm of your other hand. Fold your hand loosely around the pasta, then **twist the rod**, not the dough, to detach it. Slide it out and proudly lay your ringlet of pasta on the tray. Repeat until the dough is all used up.

Fileja alla Silana

Pasta with Sausage and Porcini

For a few months in the autumn fresh *porcini* are plentiful here. I can even buy them in my local supermarket. What a treat! The rest of the year they're frozen, again from the supermarket, or dried, which is what I use most of the time. They add a deep, savoury richness to the classic southern blend of tomato, sausage and pasta.

Serves 6

1 quantity of fresh *fileja* (see page 228), or 450–550g
    dried bucatini or fusilli
freshly grated smoked ricotta or pecorino, to serve

For the sauce
40g dried *porcini*
400g pure pork sausages
1 onion, chopped
3 cloves of garlic, chopped
3 tablespoons extra virgin olive oil
450g passata
3 tablespoons finely chopped parsley
1 teaspoon dried oregano
salt and freshly ground black pepper

Pour 400ml of boiling water over the dried *porcini* and leave to soak for half an hour or so. Once they are soft, lift them out with a fork or your fingers, leaving the soaking water and grit in the bowl. If the pieces are large, cut them into thick strips. Let it settle, then carefully pour the water off and reserve, leaving the grit behind. Slit the sausages open lengthways, peel away and discard the skin, then crumble the sausage meat as best you can.

Put the chopped onion and garlic into a roomy saucepan with the olive oil. Set over a low-moderate heat and fry gently for 5–10 minutes, until translucent. Raise the heat and add the *porcini*. Fry briskly for another 4–5 minutes, until beginning to colour here and there. Tip in the sausage meat and carry on frying until it has lost all its rawness. Pour in the reserved mushroom water and the passata, and add the parsley, oregano, salt and freshly ground black pepper. Cover and simmer everything together gently for half an hour, stirring occasionally. Add a splash of water if it gets too thick. Taste and adjust the seasoning.

Boil the pasta in plenty of salted water until almost, but not quite, al dente. With fresh pasta this will take just 3–5 minutes, depending on how much it has dried out before cooking. With bought pasta, follow the guidelines on the packet, reducing the time by 1 minute. Scoop a mugful of the cooking water out before draining the pasta. As it cooks, heat the sauce up if necessary. Tip the drained pasta into the sauce. Mix together swiftly, adding a slurp or two of the pasta water if you think it needs it. Serve *prontissimo*, with grated cheese.

Patate 'Mpacchiuse

Stoved Potatoes and Onions

Nearly all the restaurants in Camigliatello list *patate 'mpacchi-use* on their menus, showing off the famous Sila potatoes with their waxy texture. The ingredients are simple, just potatoes, onions, olive oil and salt, but it helps to have a heavy cast-iron pan to cook them in. If you get the method right, you will end up with a gorgeous, irresistible mound of soft potatoes and onions, mixed with the browned semi-fried potato from the bottom of the pan. Flaky British sea salt makes this extra good.

Serves 4

900g large end-of-season new potatoes, or other waxy
    potatoes, peeled
4 tablespoons extra virgin olive oil
salt
1 onion, thinly sliced

Slice the potatoes very thinly. Spoon the olive oil into a 24–27cm heavy-based frying pan, with a lid. Heat well, then add the potatoes. Smooth them down, then sprinkle with salt. Lower the heat, cover tightly and leave to cook without interference for 10 minutes. Uncover, turn the potatoes, then spread the onion over the top. Season again with salt. Cover and let the whole lot cook over a gentle heat for another 15 minutes.

Uncover and use a fish slice or a large spoon to carefully mix the potatoes and onion. Return to the heat and carry on cooking for another 10 minutes or so, uncovered, until the potatoes and onion are blissfully tender and browned underneath. Taste and add a little more salt if needed, then serve.

Run for the Hills

There it is, behind the glass recycling bin, a dramatic mural that could have been painted from a still from *Game of Thrones*. A dashing grim-faced hero on a milk-white stallion, brandishing his curved sword, red cloak streaming from his shoulders. It isn't, but it totally could be. This is Skanderbeg, the great Albanian hero who turned tables on the land-hungry Ottoman Empire way back in the fifteenth century. As a youth he had been sent as a hostage to the Ottoman Turkish court, where he was educated and trained in the arts of warfare. After twenty years of kowtowing to the sultan, he declared his true allegiance, which was, of course, to his home country, Albania, and his people. He led his troops bravely and regained much lost territory until his death in 1468.

Then things went decidedly pear-shaped. The Ottoman forces battled and ransacked and slaughtered and pillaged their way back through Albania. Thousands of Albanians fled across the Adriatic to the safer shores of Italy. A few settled in Puglia, more fled for safety to the hills of Basilicata and in particular, Calabria. Five and a half centuries later, their descendants are still there and much of their culture has survived.

Civita, on the edge of the vast Polino nature reserve, is one of thirty-three small Calabrian towns and villages where an Arbëreshë (Albanian) dialect is still spoken by many of the inhabitants. As well as the colourful Skanderbeg mural, there's a huge, disturbingly stern bust of the hero in the centre of town. Street signs are written in Arbëreshë and Italian and the interior of the main church, the Chiesa Santa Maria Assunta, is a-glimmer with hundreds of gold-leaf-encrusted icons.

There are some really strange forms of pasta here. *I dromesat* are small crumbs of pasta, usually cooked directly in sauce, made by dipping a bunch of dried oregano in water and shaking it over the flour. *I shtridhelat*, on the other hand, is stretched and looped and stretched and looped longer, and longer and longer, to form hefty skeins of pasta rope. Very impressive and the kind of thing that takes years to perfect.

Another trace of the Albanian ancestry is a fondness for a savoury breakfast, which is so not typical of Italy. At my B&B in the shadow of La Sentinella cliff, Mariana serves a breakfast feast with fried egg on phenomenally good, chewy bread alongside cheeses and thick yoghurt, echoing the flavours of the Eastern Mediterranean. More Italian-style cakes and pastries are plentiful too. Later at La Kamastra restaurant I get the same vibe, as I eat the tender kid goat roast slowly in the oven, after a big plate of home-made maccheroni with wild boar sauce. A synthesis of two cultures that take their food very seriously.

Tumact Me Tulez

Tagliatelle with Walnuts, Tomato and Anchovies

This is one of the most renowned Arbëreshë pasta dishes – it has a festival all of its own in the town of Barile in Basilicata. No wonder, for it is an absolute winner. There's an unusual roster of ingredients, with walnuts, anchovies, tomatoes and breadcrumbs, but something magic happens when they come together.

Serves 4

170g crustless bread, torn into small bits
2 tablespoons chopped parsley
4 cloves of garlic, chopped
5 tablespoons extra virgin olive oil
100g walnuts, chopped fairly finely
350g tagliatelle
45g anchovy fillets, chopped
1 x 400g tin of chopped tomatoes
salt, if needed, and freshly ground black pepper

Process the bread with one-third of the parsley and a quarter of the garlic to form fine breadcrumbs. Put 3 tablespoons of olive oil into a wide frying pan, add the breadcrumbs and place over a moderate heat. Stir more or less continuously until the breadcrumbs are lightly browned. Pile in the chopped walnuts and cook for a minute or so longer. Scrape out into a bowl. Wipe the pan clean with kitchen paper (no need to wash it) so that it is ready for the tomato sauce.

Bring a large pan of salted water up to the boil. Add the pasta, stir and leave to cook until just al dente.

Meanwhile, spoon the remaining 2 tablespoons of olive oil into the frying pan and add the remaining garlic and the anchovies. Place over a moderate heat and fry, mashing down the anchovies, until the garlic is lightly coloured and the anchovies have roughly dissolved. Tip in the tomatoes, add most of the remaining parsley (save a little to add colour when serving) and plenty of freshly ground black pepper, and simmer for 5–10 minutes. If it looks a tad dry, scoop in a ladleful of the pasta cooking water. Stir in half the breadcrumb and walnut mixture and add a little more pasta water to make a thick sauce.

Scoop out a mugful of the pasta cooking water and reserve. Drain the pasta and tip into the frying pan. Over a generous heat, toss everything together. If it looks too dry, add an extra slurp or two of cooking water. Serve straight away, sprinkled with the remaining crisp breadcrumbs and walnuts and a scattering of parsley.

Capretto Al Forno

Roast Kid

When I asked about typical recipes in Civita, kid (as in baby goat) was the response every time. Mariana's version was cooked in a frying pan, La Kamastra's in an earthenware *tegame* (a two-handled pot which can be used stovetop or in the oven), and the man in the bar thought it should go into the oven. Seasonings were similar, the quantity of tomato varied massively. This recipe is a loose amalgam of them all, with tender, softly-flavoured kid marinated overnight with white wine, juniper and olive oil, then gently roasted.

Make sure you are buying young kid for this recipe, not fully matured goat, which requires longer, slower cooking. You may find it easiest to buy online unless your butcher can order it in for you. Ask for the meat to be cut into chunks on the bone, around 9cm long and 5cm wide.

Serves 4

1kg kid on the bone, cut into large chunks
200g cherry tomatoes, halved

For the marinade
6 tablespoons extra virgin olive oil
8 dried juniper berries, crushed
1 onion, thickly sliced
1 carrot, sliced
4 cloves of garlic, peeled and bashed
1 stem of celery, sliced
150ml white wine
salt and freshly ground black pepper

Put the kid into a large bowl with all the marinade ingredients. Mix well, then cover and leave to marinate in the fridge for 24 hours. Bring back to room temperature before cooking.

Preheat the oven to 200°C/180°C fan/gas 6. Tip the kid and all the marinade and vegetables into a roasting tin. Add the cherry tomatoes. Ideally the meat should be in a single snug layer, with no big gaps between chunks. If you can see the metal base, add a few spoonfuls of water to the pan as well, to prevent drying out. Roast for 25 minutes, then stir. There should be plenty of juice, but if not, add a splash of water. Return to the oven for a final 35–40 minutes, until the meat is lightly browned. Serve with boiled potatoes or wedges of good bread to mop up the juices.

Pasta alla Pastora

Pasta with Ricotta, Pecorino and Pancetta (or Sausage)

Finding your road blocked by a herd of goats or sheep is still a relatively common occurrence here. Sheepishly, I admit that I sometimes find it difficult to distinguish one from the other. The sheep of the *mezzogiorno* are skinny, athletic little beasts compared to the bucolic plump fluffiness of their northern cousins. Different breeds, of course, bred over centuries to deal with contrasts of summer heat and sparse greenery, interspersed with damp, chilly winters clambering up steep slopes. These are the descendants of animals that have been herded up and down mountains and hills twice a year every year by their shepherds, since forever. Well, since at least the days of the Greek colonies of Magna Graecia, nearly three thousand years ago.

Their milk goes to produce not only fine pecorino cheeses, fragrant and tender with wafts of herbiness when young, piquant and feisty when matured to grating hardness, but also the best soft creamy ricotta. Sheep's milk ricotta is one of life's little pleasures in the south of Italy. To be honest, it doesn't taste radically different to cow's milk ricotta but just edges past it, just a little creamier, just a little more purity, just a little more flavour.

I've made *pasta alla pastora* (*pastora* means either shepherdess or the shepherd's wife) with both artisan sheep's ricotta and commercial cow's ricotta. Both are delicious and all the better for the simplicity of the recipe. The flecks of green parsley are essentially no more than a visual gimmick, relieving the otherwise insistent whiteness of the pasta ricotta combo, so leave them out if you want to.

Serves 4

320–350g cavatelli, penne or fusilli
200g smoked pancetta lardons or high-quality Italian
    pork sausages, skinned and crumbled
300g ricotta
45g freshly grated pecorino
salt and freshly ground black pepper
1 tablespoon finely chopped parsley (optional)

To serve
extra freshly grated pecorino

Cook the pasta in plenty of boiling, well-salted water until just al dente.

While it cooks, put the pancetta or sausage meat into a wide frying pan and place over a moderate heat. Fry gently at first to release some of the fat, then increase the heat a little to brown the pancetta/sausage meat lightly. Take off the heat if the pasta isn't cooked yet. Meanwhile, tip the ricotta into a bowl and add a ladleful of the pasta cooking water. Stir to a cream, adding a little more water if needed. Stir in the pecorino.

Scoop out a mugful of the pasta cooking water, then drain the pasta. Tip it into the pancetta pan and set over a moderate heat. Scrape in the ricotta cream, add a generous few twists of freshly ground black pepper and toss everything together, adding a little more cooking water if needed. The cooking water, pancetta and pecorino should have brought quite enough salt to the pasta, so only add more if it really needs it. As soon as the pasta is steam-ing hot, serve, scattered with a little parsley if using, and some extra grated pecorino.

Pasta China

Baked Pasta with Meatballs, Cheese and Hot Sausage

This is the stuff of a family Sunday lunch in the south of Italy. Pasta China is the Calabrian version of homely *pasta al forno*, the equivalent of the more northerly lasagne. It's usually made with rigatoni, ridged tubes of pasta, dressed with tomato sauce, mixed with little meatballs, *caciocavallo* or *provolone* cheese, hard-boiled egg and a bit of spicy sausage. It may not be grand but it is definitely a total crowd-pleaser.

Though it is a bit of a palaver to make, you can prepare it all well in advance. Just leave the final baking in the oven until shortly before serving.

Serves 8

500g rigatoni or penne
3 eggs
100–150g *'nduja* or 200g spicy salami, diced
200g *caciocavallo stagionato*, or *provolone piccante*
a good handful of basil leaves, roughly shredded
3 tablespoons freshly grated pecorino or Parmesan

For the tomato sauce
1 onion, chopped
3 cloves of garlic, chopped
3 tablespoons extra virgin olive oil
1.2 litres passata
salt and freshly ground black pepper

For the meatballs
200g minced beef or pork or veal
50g soft breadcrumbs
50g freshly grated pecorino or Parmesan
1 heaped tablespoon finely chopped parsley
salt and freshly ground black pepper
1 egg, beaten
1 tablespoon extra virgin olive oil

Begin by making the tomato sauce. Put the onion, garlic and olive oil into a large saucepan. Cook over a gentle heat, stirring occasionally, without browning, until the onion is tender and translucent. Add the passata, 250ml of water, salt and freshly ground black pepper and bring up to the boil. Turn the heat down again, three-quarters cover the pan with a lid, and let the sauce simmer gently for at least half an hour. Stir occasionally, scraping the bottom of the pan so that the sauce doesn't catch. Taste and adjust the seasoning.

Make the meatballs while the sauce simmers. Put all the ingredients except the egg and oil into a bowl. Add about two-thirds of the egg. Mix the ingredients together thoroughly with your hands, squeezing and working the mixture until it holds together. Break off small knobs of the mixture and roll to form meatballs approximately 1½cm in diameter. Heat the olive oil in a wide frying pan over a high heat. Tip in the meatballs and fry until patched with brown all over. Spoon out on to a plate and reserve.

Now the pasta. Bring a large pan of well-salted water to the boil. Tip in the rigatoni or penne, stir, then add the eggs to the pan too. Bring back to the boil. After 9 minutes, lift out the eggs and plunge them into a bowl of cold water. Taste the pasta. It needs to be a fraction shy of al dente, i.e. a little chewier than you would ultimately like it to be. Drain.

Preheat the oven to 190°C/170°C fan/gas 5. Shell the eggs and slice. Mix with the pasta, the tomato sauce, the meatballs, the *'nduja* broken into small knobs or the diced salami, the *cacio-cavallo* or *provolone* and the basil. Tip into a baking dish, smooth down as best you can, then dredge with the grated pecorino or Parmesan. Bake for 20 minutes if the ingredients are still warm, or around 30 minutes if they are cold. Serve piping hot from the oven.

Pythagoras, Theorems and Beans

I'm guessing that I first came across the Pythagoras theorem when I was around ten or eleven years old. It is handsomely neat and tidy, both surprising and satisfying, and may well have had something to do with my subsequent fondness for maths. At the time its progenitor was not so interesting. Some fusty ancient Greek dude who probably had a white beard and a toga and was therefore eminently unmemorable.

These past few months, as I've tootled along the Ionian instep, he pogos up on my radar with conspicuous regularity. In his time, some two and a half millennia ago, he was definitely a big cheese around the coastal plains of Basilicata and Calabria. He founded his philosophical school of acolytes in the Greek city of Crotone, welcoming in women as much as men, which was quite something back then. Later he may probably or may not equally probably have decamped to the equally Greek city of Metaponto, slap bang on what is now the border with Puglia. The columns of Metaponto's magnificent Temple of Hera, queen of the gods, rise up among the trees, alongside the dual carriageway. Infuriatingly, the iron gates have been firmly chained and locked every time I've attempted to visit, but that's Italy for you. Closed for lunch, closed for the winter, closed for holidays, closed for restoration work. It can be very frustrating.

As it turns out, there has been endless and voluminous debate among historians about what Pythagoras actually did or believed or said, or indeed whether he ever genuinely made it to Metaponto. Most accounts of his life were written long after his death, and most of them clash and waver on the detail. Some points of agreement – he was born in Samos, he came to Crotone when he was around forty years old. He believed in a pure, unindulgent lifestyle and insisted on a mostly plant-based quasi-vegetarian diet. He expected his students to do the same. He was firmly anti democracy. He never, ever ate broad beans. The more I learn about him, the less I like him.

Pythagoras's loathing for and fear of broad beans (*fava* here in Italy as well as in the USA) was (possibly) based on a belief that they housed the souls of the dead. Or another that they increased wind, which expelled some of the 'breath of life'. Perhaps more plausible is that he was one of the unfortunate individuals who suffer from favism. Favism is a genetically inherited disease, most common around the Mediterranean, which is sparked by the ingestion of a number of medicines and foods, particularly broad beans and blueberries, inducing a form of jaundice. In my local supermarket, fresh broad beans are labelled with a big warning that they may cause illness to those who suffer from favism.

Eventually the burghers of Crotone turned against Pythagoras. They set fire to his school and he and his henchmen fled the city. According to a number of chroniclers, his helter-skelter escape through farmlands, toga hitched up high, led him straight towards a field of broad beans. It brought him to a juddering standstill, too horrified to plough through them. A fatal error. His incandescent pursuers caught up with him and slashed him to the ground. And that, dear reader, was the ignominious end of Pythagoras.

In this version of history, it was just his followers who made it to Metapontum and set up a school in his memory. Whatever. He still made a remarkable contribution to the mathematical canon with his theorem . . . or maybe he didn't. As it happens, the ancient Babylonians knew all about the square on the hypotenuse centuries before Pythagoras was the teensiest twinkle in his mater's eye. Damn it, this man is such a disappointment. Thank heavens, then, that the poor, uneducated hoi polloi of southern Italy have not espoused his broad bean beliefs. From Puglia with its excellent dish of *fave alle cicoria*, through Basilicata and Calabria, broad beans, fresh in season, dried throughout the rest of the year, are still eaten with unpythagorian gusto.

Ditaloni Rigati con Fave Fresche, Finocchio, Pancetta

Pasta with Broad Beans, Fennel and Pancetta

When spring hits and the first broad beans start to pile up on market stalls, much of Italy will be found tucking into a plate of pasta and *fave* of a lunchtime. It's a dish I first encountered in Sicily a long time ago and it soon became part of my home repertoire. Coming across it again in the wilds of Calabria reminded me that broad beans, pancetta and pecorino are among the happiest of *menages à trois*. Adding a good handful of wild fennel leaves, as they do here, makes it even more delicious.

For all that it is a simple dish, quickly cooked, it does demand a degree of patience. Shelling broad beans of a leisurely afternoon, perhaps with a friend or a congenial relative, a lover or a good audio book, can be a time of contented pleasure. Naturally, the sun will be shining, the world will be at peace, you will be sitting in a warm but not overheated spot with just the right amount of dappled shade, a pitcher of lemonade or a glass of chilled white wine close at hand. Idyllic. On the other hand, when the usual mini-crises of daily life are bubbling around you and that cup of tea you made half an hour ago remains half-drunk and cold, the prospect of shelling a mountain of broad beans is a pain in the posterior.

The thing is that though undoubtedly very fresh broad beans are going to taste best, especially when they are young, small and sweet, frozen broad beans are damn fine. Especially when I break it to you that this spring dish of pasta with beans and bacon will taste so much better if you peel the skin off at least half the individual beans. That's another fifteen minutes of pre-prep. Sorry, but it really does make a big difference.

Serves 4

2kg fresh broad beans in the pod, or 350–400g shelled
    broad beans, fresh or frozen
350–400g *ditaloni rigati* or conchiglie
3 tablespoons extra virgin olive oil
1 red onion, chopped
200g pancetta lardons
2 cloves of garlic, chopped
a small bunch of fennel or dill leaves, chopped
salt and freshly ground black pepper

To serve
freshly grated pecorino or Parmesan

Begin with the beans. If in the pod, crack them open and extract the beans. Bring a pan of salted water to the boil and add the beans, fresh or frozen. Boil for 1 minute, then drain and run under the cold tap. As soon as they are cool enough to handle, pop as many of the bright green inner beanlets out of their grey shell as you can be bothered to – I reckon that you need to do at least half of them, but more is better.

Put a large pan of well-salted water on to boil. Pour in the pasta when it reaches a rolling boil and cook until almost but not quite al dente. Scoop out a mugful of the cooking water, then drain.

Meanwhile, put the olive oil, onion, pancetta and garlic into a wide frying pan. Set over a moderate heat and fry gently, until the onion is tender and translucent. Tip in the broad beans and the fennel or dill. Season with a little salt and lots of freshly ground black pepper. Swish about for a minute or so to coat them in the oil. Now add a ladleful of the cooking water from the pasta, cover with a lid and leave to simmer for 3–4 minutes, until the beans are tender.

Tip the pasta into the frying pan. Toss with the beans and pancetta, adding a little more cooking water if it seems dry. Serve straight away, with freshly grated pecorino or Parmesan.

Three Pasta and Cuttlefish Recipes with Similar Ingredients and Divergent Outcomes

For many years, for no good reason as it turns out, I've sub-consciously considered cuttlefish the poor second cousin to squid. Now I know better. Thank you, Puglia, Basilicata and Calabria, for knocking this foolishness away. As with all long-held beliefs, one should always be willing to dust them off and check the foundations to see if they are worth clutching on to. See also my late-in-life conversion to *tiramisù* (page 83). Cuttlefish is my new tip-top seafood, for the moment at least.

A cursory glance at the fishmongers, and squid and cuttle-fish look similar, especially when they've been cleaned. They are both cephalopods, a word that derives from the delight-fully descriptive ancient Greek for 'feet on the head', both relatives of the similarly foot-challenged much larger octopus. The cuttlefish's 'feet' are on the short side compared with its cousins, but the body has a sturdiness and sweetness that marks it out. The freshest cuttlefish, uncleaned, stand out like the most exotic of animals on the fishmonger's slab, a marine zebra reimagined by Picasso.

All along Italy's southern coasts, impeccably fresh cut-tlefish are eaten raw. A *tagliatelle di seppie* isn't a pasta dish at all, but a tangle of strips of raw cuttlefish, dressed at the last minute with olive oil and sometimes a squeeze or two of lemon juice. At its best the milk-white flesh is as smooth as satin, a sweet creamy burst of deliciousness.

If you are going to cook cuttlefish you must either opt for the briefest exposure to a high heat, or commit to long slow braising. The end results are entirely different but both are a pleasure to eat, every bit as good as common cousin squid, if not rather better. Versions of all three of these cuttlefish dishes are cooked right through Italy's instep as well as in Sicily. This first is the simplest, the second, with the addition of black ink, is certainly the most dramatic, while the third is the get-ahead version, best cooked up to a day in advance and ripe for thorough reheating shortly before tossing with your pasta.

Buying Cuttlefish

Some fishmongers sell cuttlefish already cleaned and pearly white, others display them as they come, stripy skin and all. Though the latter will probably clean them for you if you ask nicely, they are really not so difficult to deal with at home, with the added bonus that you may be able to extract the ink sac to use in your pasta sauce or indeed to pen an old-fashioned letter with – the word sepia comes from the Italian for cuttlefish, *seppia*. You will also be the recipient of one or more cuttle bones, so beloved of budgies.

Pre-cleaned or not, the priority will be freshness. Let your instinct guide you. The white flesh or the whole body must be glistening, plump and healthy-looking, with not the slightest hint of a whiff to it. If the poor things look wan, jet-lagged and miserable, if there is a minim of a nose-wrinkling odour, turn your back and rethink your menu.

Ideally, you would like to be taking home medium-sized cuttlefish – that's somewhere around 150–200g each – but in reality, you will just have to take whatever is available. Big cuttlefish will be thicker-fleshed and a little chewier, so slice them thinner and be doubly sure to either flash-fry them at a spanking heat or allow extra time to braise them nice and slow.

An inky aside: Both squid and cuttlefish employ an inspired dark invisibility cloak when they are threatened, diving away from predators through waters blackened by their own ink. For us human predators, this murky ink is a blessed bonus, adding not just a shot of sheer drama to food, but also a shot of profound flavour. However, you can't bank on cuttlefish's internal ink sacs being fully intact by the time they get to your kitchen. Even when they haven't ejected a cloud of ink as they are caught, the sac is easily ruptured along the journey from boat to marble display slab, or even more annoyingly when you are cleaning the fish itself. Frankly, it makes sense to buy a sachet of pasteurised cuttlefish or squid ink as a back-up while you are at the fishmonger's. It keeps for months if you don't use it straight away.

How to clean a cuttlefish

Cleaning your own cuttlefish is fascinating, and if you are lucky you may be able to harvest your own cuttlefish ink. There are plenty of helpful how-to videos on YouTube, but here are my step-by-step instructions on how to tackle it. They make far more sense when you actually have the cuttlefish in front of you on the chopping board. Be warned, it can be a messy job but it's also deeply satisfying.

1. Gather a bowl of cold water (essential for rinsing your hands and the cuttlefish as you work), kitchen towel, a sharp knife and a glass or small bowl (for the ink sacs) beside your chopping board.

2. Lay the cuttlefish on the board with the paler side down. Prod the upper side with your fingers to locate the surfboard-shaped cuttlebone. Using a small sharp knife, cut down on either side of it, then slip the bone out. It's a strange and fascinating thing – a calcified sponge that the cuttlefish pumps with gas to make it buoyant or liquid when it wants to sink down towards the sea bed. If you have chickens or a pet bird, clean it thoroughly and give it to them; if not, chuck it in the bin.

3. Use your fingers to work the innards, head and tentacles out and away from the main body. If the ink sac has been broken this will be a messy, inky-black undertaking. If it is intact, it will still be messy, but not so much. In the latter case take great care not to rupture the black ink sac.

4. Grasp one of the 'wings' on the main body and pull it off firmly, gradually tugging away the tough skin that covers the rest of the body. If the wings are large enough to make a decent mouthful, peel the skin away from them. Discard the skin. Rinse the body in the cold water.

5. If you are intending to stuff the cuttlefish, leave the body as it is. Otherwise, slice in half lengthways, then cut into strips or squares.

6. Now back to the head and innards. Slice the tentacles off, just above the eyes. Check the centre and remove the hard beak if it is still lurking there. Toss the tentacles on to the pile of prepared cuttlefish. Examine the rest. If the black pouch of ink looks intact, carefully cut and ease it out and drop it into the glass. Throw all the rest out.

7. Clean everything up before you get dark sepia splashes of ink over your entire kitchen.

Spaghetti alla Seppia

Spaghetti with Cuttlefish

Fast and simple, this is a beautiful way to show off cuttlefish. With all the ingredients prepared and ready to go, the actual cooking can be done in less time than it takes to boil dried pasta.

Serves 4

350g spaghetti or tagliolini (fine tagliatelle) or linguine
3 tablespoons extra virgin olive oil
500g cuttlefish, cleaned and cut into thin strips
3 cloves of garlic, chopped
1 red chilli, fresh or dried, finely chopped (optional)
12 cherry tomatoes, quartered
150ml dry white wine
salt and freshly ground black pepper
3 tablespoons chopped parsley

Cook the spaghetti in boiling salted water until just al dente.

Meanwhile, heat the olive oil in a wide frying pan over a high heat. Add the cuttlefish and fry for 1 minute, tossing in the hot oil. Scoop them out on to a plate. Now add the garlic and chilli, if using, to the pan and fry for a few seconds, until beginning to colour. Add the cherry tomatoes and fry for another minute or two, until beginning to soften. Pour in the wine, season with salt and freshly ground black pepper and sizzle it away until reduced by half. Now add the parsley and a ladleful of the pasta cooking water. Simmer for a minute or two, then return the cuttlefish to the pan. Using a pair of tongs, lift the spaghetti out of its cooking water straight into the pan. Toss for a minute or so with the sauce and the cuttlefish, keeping the heat high until the pasta has absorbed most of the liquid.

Serve immediately.

Spaghetti al Nero di Seppia
Black Spaghetti with Cuttlefish

As Spaghetti alla Seppia, but add the ink from 1 or 2 ink sacs, or 1 x 4g sachet of pasteurised cuttlefish ink, to the frying pan with the first ladle of pasta water. Marvel at the power of that small squirt of ink, as the entire contents of the pan disappears into a mound of sheer blackness. Serve swiftly, possibly with a sprinkling of chopped parsley or fresh chilli if you need to alleviate the funereal depths.

Spaghetti al Sugo di Seppie e Piselli

Spaghetti with Slow-Cooked Cuttlefish and Peas

Here the cuttlefish is cooked down gently in its wine-spiked tomato *sugo*. The flavour is quite different, fuller and more rounded.

Serves 4

350g spaghetti or tagliolini (fine tagliatelle)

For the sauce
3 tablespoons extra virgin olive oil
1 onion, finely chopped
3 cloves of garlic, finely chopped
1–2 red chillies, chopped
1 bay leaf
2 tablespoons finely chopped parsley
2 generous sprigs of thyme
500g cuttlefish, cleaned and sliced
150ml dry white wine
700g passata
salt and freshly ground black pepper
150g shelled peas (frozen is fine)

Make the sauce in advance – it needs plenty of gentle simmering to get that cuttlefish über-tender. Start by placing the olive oil, onion, garlic, chillies, bay leaf, parsley and thyme in a saucepan. Set over a moderate heat and fry gently, stirring occasionally, until the onion is translucent and soft. Don't rush it – we're looking at a good 10 minutes or more of gentle cooking.

Now raise the heat and add the cuttlefish to the pan. Fry briefly, then pour in the wine and let it sizzle for a minute or two. Add the passata and season with salt and freshly ground black pepper. Bring to the boil, then reduce the heat, half cover with a lid, and simmer gently for at least 1 hour, stirring occasionally. Add a splash of water every now and then if the sauce threatens to catch. Check the cuttlefish – by now it should be beautifully tender. This cuttlefish stew can be cooled and stored in the fridge for up to 24 hours if it makes life easier.

Put a large pan of well-salted water on to boil. Once boiling hard, add the pasta and cook until just al dente. Meanwhile, reheat the sauce thoroughly. Stir in the peas and simmer for a couple more minutes. Drain the pasta, reserving a mugful of the cooking water. Toss with the hot sauce, adding a slurp or two of pasta water if necessary to help the sauce coat the strands of spaghetti evenly. Serve right away.

Afterthought on cooking cuttlefish

Forget the pasta and wine for a moment. When all I want is a straightforward, right-now plate of cuttlefish for dinner, I buy it ready-cleaned, bathe it in a quick marinade of olive oil, lemon juice, chopped garlic, chopped parsley and chilli, salt and freshly ground black pepper for 30–60 minutes, then griddle or barbecue it over a monstrously hot heat for no more than a minute on each side. Fast food doesn't get much better.

Swordfish in Dire Straits

On a couple of occasions, back in the '80s, I took the overnight train down from Rome to Palermo. My patchy sleep was shaken off in the early morning by the strange to-and-fro motion of the train loading on to the ferry, ready to chug across the Straits of Messina to Sicily. In the half-light the carriages were shunted on a few at a time, a slow and laborious procedure that was repeated in reverse after the short ride across the six and a half kilometres of sea separating Sicily from Calabria. Over the intervening decades little has changed – the latest ferries are battery-operated, systems are slicker, but the essential process is just the same. Dreams of constructing a road and rail bridge have come and gone over the centuries. It was first proposed by a Roman consul some time in the third century BC. Italy's current prime minister, Giorgia Meloni, has once again announced plans to build a 3.3 kilometre single-span bridge across the narrowest part of the straits, linking the two regions. This is an idea that has met with animated, often vitriolic debate. Will it see the light of day? Will it really happen this time? Will the train ferry puff its last gasp? Only time will tell.

Pre-dating the ferries is a far more ancient form of boat – the unique *spadara* or felucca. This is the classic swordfishing craft that plies the straits, searching for the swift streaks of silver-grey fish. At the centre of each boat, a tall tower where the lookout waits for a sighting. At the front, the long *passerella* juts out over the water. A harpoonist stands at its tip waiting for prey to pass, unsuspecting, underneath. Like the train ferry, the feluccas' future is in doubt. Once there were dozens of them fishing plentiful swordfish one by sustainable one. These days, the swordfish have been over-fished by dragnets (now banned) and drifting longline systems. In the forty or so years since I first took the overnight train from Rome to the south, Mediterranean swordfish stocks have dropped by some 80%.

Reluctantly, as I love swordfish, I no longer eat it in restaurants in Italy and I won't cook it at home unless my fishmonger can guarantee, in a most un-Italian way, that it comes from some more sustainable source in another part of the world.

Pesce Spada alla Ghiotta

Swordfish with Potatoes, Tomato, Capers and Olives

Ghiotta is a word with many meanings – it's usually translated as greedy, but might, more pleasingly, mean something wonderful, delicious, a treat. *Pesce spada* (or any other firm white fish) *alla ghiotta* is something of a treat, one that might be found anywhere along the coastal tip of Italy's toe or in eastern Sicily. Make the sauce in advance, ready to spoon over the swiftly cooked fish.

If you can't get sustainably sourced swordfish, the recipe works well with hake steaks, which tend to be thicker than swordfish so will require an extra couple of minutes' cooking time.

Serves 4

400g potatoes, cut into 2cm cubes
1 onion, chopped
2 cloves of garlic, thinly sliced
1 red chilli, fresh or dried, finely chopped
4 tablespoons extra virgin olive oil
1 x 400g tin of chopped tomatoes
salt and freshly ground black pepper
2 tablespoons capers, rinsed if salted
60g black olives, stoned and sliced
a good handful of basil leaves, roughly shredded
600g sustainable swordfish steaks, cut about 1cm thick

Boil the potatoes in salted water for about 5 minutes, until barely cooked through. Drain and reserve.

Put the onion, garlic, chilli and 3 tablespoons of olive oil into a heavy-based frying pan. Set over a moderate heat and leave to cook gently for at least 10 minutes, until the onion is translucent and tender. Tip in the tomatoes, add about 200ml of water and season with salt and freshly ground black pepper. Simmer together for 15–20 minutes. Stir in the potatoes, capers, olives and basil leaves. Simmer for a couple more minutes, then take off the heat while you cook the swordfish steaks.

Preheat a heavy griddle pan or heavy-based frying pan over a generous heat. Pat the swordfish dry with kitchen paper, divide it into 4 pieces, then brush on both sides with the remaining oil. Lay the swordfish in the hot pan. Cook for 2–3 minutes on each side (or a little longer if necessary), until just cooked through. Reheat the sauce if necessary. Top the swordfish steaks with the sauce and serve at once.

Tonno in Agrodolce

Seared Tuna with Sweet-Sour Onions, Mint and Pinenuts

As you mosey along the coastline between Taranto and Reggio Calabria, diving in and out of the interior lands, a new set of flavours begins to amble into meals. Somewhere around Crotone or perhaps Catanzaro comes the first hint of *agrodolce*, sweet and sour. Slow-cooked onions, sweet and sharp with vinegar, lively with the breeze of mint, are unexpectedly delicious piled on to a tuna steak. In the classic version, the tuna is cubed, floured, fried and over-cooked. I prefer this more modern version, with swiftly seared tuna still a little pink at heart.

Serves 2–3

350–400g fresh tuna steak, cut around 2cm thick
1 clove of garlic, halved
juice of ½ a lemon
extra virgin olive oil
20g pinenuts

For the onions
2 red onions, thinly sliced
2 tablespoons extra virgin olive oil
1 tablespoon red wine vinegar
1 tablespoon caster sugar
salt and freshly ground black pepper
2 tablespoons water
leaves from 2 sprigs of mint, roughly torn up

Put the onions and olive oil into a saucepan. Place over a low heat and cover, then leave to cook for about 10–15 minutes, stirring occasionally, until the onions are floppy and tender. Stir in the vinegar, caster sugar, salt, freshly ground black pepper and water. Simmer together for another 2 minutes or so, until most, but not all, of the liquid has disappeared. Reserve a few torn mint leaves and stir the rest into the onions.

About half an hour before you want to serve the tuna, rub both sides of the steak with the halved clove of garlic. Squeeze over the lemon juice and drizzle with olive oil, then season with salt and freshly ground black pepper. Turn the steaks a couple of times and set aside. Dry-fry the pinenuts until golden brown.

To cook the tuna, preheat an oiled griddle pan or heavy-based frying pan over a high heat for 4–5 minutes, until outrageously hot. Lay the tuna steak in the pan and cook for 1 minute without moving it. Turn it over and cook for 1 more minute on the other side. As it cooks, reheat the onions gently.

Place the tuna on a serving dish and top with the onions. Scatter with the pinenuts and reserved mint leaves. Serve immediately.

A Mad Dinner Party

There was a table set out under a tree in front of the house, and the March Hare and the Hatter were having tea at it: a Dormouse was sitting between them, fast asleep, and the other two were using it as a cushion, resting their elbows on it, and talking over its head. 'Very uncomfortable for the Dormouse,' thought Alice; 'only, as it's asleep, I suppose it doesn't mind.'
– Lewis Carroll, *Alice in Wonderland*

I have tried, on the whole, to avoid gratuitous mention of the mafia. This is a cookery book, after all. Thankfully they do not impinge directly on my everyday life, but that they exist in the shadows is undeniable. They emerge into the media spotlight once in a while, then steal back into the dark unsavoury voids. Stories abound about what and who they control, the buildings they own, how they launder their money. It takes a far braver soul than I to delve down to the extortion, drug deals, threats and murders.

Small-scale corruption lurks just under the surface everywhere here. If you want to get things done, it helps big time to know the right person who will tug the relevant string of a planning department or the hospital admissions office. At least two nearby towns have had their town councils dissolved when the string-pulling spilled over into something more pernicious.

Puglia has its own crime syndicate, the Sacra Corona Unita, but they are small fry compared to Calabria's infamous 'Ndrangheta, whose sinewy tentacles slither out around the world. Reputedly they control some 80% of Europe's cocaine trade, among their many other businesses. They are a pretty nasty bunch, by all accounts.

The 'Ndrangheta is made up of *'ndrine*, family clans bound closely by oaths of silence and violence. Special events, inductions, clan meetings, celebrations are, of course, marked by copious feasts with lavish spreads of food and lakes of wine and beer. Top of the menu are plump, succulent, bony little dormice, fried, roast or simmered in a rich tomato sauce.

Ghiri, edible dormice, are cute little things when they are alive, with long shaggy tails that trail out behind them. Nose to fluffy tail tip they measure around 30cm. They are nocturnal creatures and hibernate through the winter months. Despite their name (from the Anglo-Norman *dormeus*, sleepy head) and snoozy reputation, they sleep no more than many similar rodents.

Lewis Carroll's dormouse was probably a hazelnut dormouse, the only variety native to the UK. Edible dormice belong to mainland Europe, though there is a small population hidden in the undergrowth in the area around Tring in Hertfordshire. They were introduced in 1902 by Walter Rothschild to the grounds of the family estate, Tring Park. Though insignificant compared to the zebras and kangaroos he kept as pets, the dormice are the ones who made a permanent home here, escaping into the parkland to establish themselves in ever increasing numbers.

The Italian taste for dormice goes way back to the Romans (and the Etruscans before them), who bred them for the table, fattening them up in the darkness of ingeniously constructed, airily ventilated clay pots called *gliraria*. These days the 'Ndrangheta's favourite restaurateurs still fatten them up, though in cages rather than clay pots. The big difference is that nowadays dormice are legally protected, not that their mafia clientele will care a jot about that.

A couple of years ago, a drugs raid in the small Calabrian town of Delianuova revealed not only a thriving cannabis plantation, but also a stash of oven-ready dormice in the freezer. They had been nicely plumped up before despatch, skinned and neatly packaged, side by side in plastic containers: 235 of them, not to mention a few more live dormice in their cages. Each small corpse is a perfectly proportioned single portion that fits on a dinner plate, little paws splayed out in final submission. About as inviting, I'd have thought, as the casserole of small songbirds, complete with heads and claws, that a lovely neighbour of mine recently proffered with an invitation to stay to lunch. I was, genuinely and thankfully, busy that afternoon. Intrepid eater I may be, but that was a step too far.

A Roman recipe for dormice

From Apicius' *De Re Coquinaria*

Stuff the dormouse with a forcemeat of finely minced pork and dormouse trimmings, blended with pepper, nuts, fennel extract and broth. Put the stuffed dormouse in an earthenware dish and roast in the oven or boil it in a casserole.

Pitta, *pidde*, *pittule*, pizza, *petole* – how to keep an etymologist occupied for an eternity

For someone arriving from a land with a clear and unperturbed appreciation of what a pitta bread is – i.e. a neat oval pocket of dough just begging to be filled with lunch of some sort – the southern Italian lexicon of derivations and meanings thereof is baffling. To me, pitta or possibly pita bread was something that emanated originally, rather vaguely, from Eastern Europe and North Africa, though probably baked and packaged in a commercial bakery in an industrial estate in Dunstable or Bolton. That English has co-opted the word from the Greek is about the only solid certainty.

Life in Puglia and travels through Basilicata and Calabria have taught me an altogether new and often confused appreciation of the edible possibilities emanating from one simple word. The common element seems to be not so much the dough but the hot oven (with the exception of *pittule*). In Italy, as in North Africa, communal ovens, or the village baker's oven, was where every household took their bread to bake. The first intense heat was perfect for thinner breads – the pitta, the pizza, et al. – while larger loaves cooked more slowly as the heat diminished. Each community had its own conventions for distinguishing one person's flatbread/loaf from the other. In Matera's Sassi (labyrinthine cave districts, once notorious slums until the 1960s, now awash with chic hotels, restaurants and shops), wooden bread-stamps, some incredibly ornate, were given as wedding gifts. Elsewhere it might be no more than a slashed pattern or initials in the dough.

Each time I try to trace some sort of logical route for the Italian derivations of the word 'pitta', I flail in a labyrinthine maze of factoids and contradictions. So instead I am guessing that Greek and Arabic settlers begat the trend. From there, the names meander away, changed through usage and dialect from cook to cook, village to village, town to town. Pittas, pies and pizzas galore. So, here then are just a few of the variants I've come across:

Pizza, obviously: The greatest of all Italian flatbreads, pride of Naples and now of all Italians the world over.

Puccia: Round, pocketed flatbreads beloved of Puglians, thicker than a conventional pitta bread, but so similar in nature and function.

Pizzata or *pane pizzata*: Calabrian cornmeal bread also known as *'ndianu*.

Pitta di San Martino (again but totally different): Chocolate-covered biscuits (recipe on page 274).

Pitta Calabrese: A wheel of bread, much eaten in the south of Calabria, often stuffed.

Pizzica rustica: From the southern Salento area of Puglia, a flat yeasted pastry filled with tomato, onion and various other fillings, known as a *focaccia ripiena* in other parts of the south.

Pizza (again but totally different) *di patate*: A potato pie from Puglia.

Pizza (again but totally different) *di ricotta*: A sweet baked ricotta cheesecake.

Pitta (again but totally different) *'mpigliata* or *'nchiusa*: Calabrian festive sweet tart packed to high heavens with dried fruit and nuts (recipe on page 271).

Pizziculova: An oval bread roll.

Pittule/pettole: Deep-fried morsels of yeasted dough, sometimes seasoned with olive, anchovy, chilli, tomato or ham, more often dusted with sugar (recipe on page 129).

La Pitta 'Mpigliata

Calabria's Fabulous, Festive Mincemeatish Tart

The *pitta 'mpigliata* is a wonderfully exuberant festive tart with whorls of pastry stuffed with nuts and booze-soaked raisins and figs. It emanates from the handsome town of San Giovanni in Fiore in Calabria, where it is rustled up to celebrate Christmas or Easter or a wedding.

Serves 12

For the pastry
500g plain flour, plus a little extra for rolling out
a pinch of salt
finely grated zest of 1 orange
100g dry white wine
100g extra virgin olive oil, plus extra for greasing
2 eggs
1 teaspoon baking powder

For the filling
100g raisins
100g dried figs, stems removed, chopped
finely grated zest and juice of 1 large orange
2 tablespoons Strega or brandy or rum
150g blanched almonds, roughly chopped
100g walnuts, roughly chopped
50g pinenuts
60g candied peel, chopped
1 teaspoon ground cinnamon
250g runny honey

Soak the raisins, figs and orange zest in the orange juice and the Strega or brandy or rum for at least 2 hours, stirring occasionally, so that most of the liquid is absorbed.

Make the pastry. Mix the flour, salt and grated orange zest. Make a well in the centre. Warm the wine and olive oil together gently, without letting them boil. Pour into the well and mix roughly. Now break in the eggs and add the baking powder. Mix to a soft dough, knead for a minute or two to smooth out, then form into 3 balls, one slightly smaller than the others. Wrap each one in clingfilm and set aside at room temperature while you finish the filling.

Add the nuts, candied peel and cinnamon to the soaked fruit. Heat the honey gently until runny, then mix in. Base-line a 23cm shallow springform cake tin with baking parchment. Brush the sides lightly with a little olive oil.

Preheat the oven to 180°C/160°C fan/gas 4. Turn back to the pastry. Take the smaller ball and roll it out on a lightly floured surface to form a thin circle about 27cm in diameter. Line the cake tin with the pastry – don't worry about trimming the edges perfectly.

Roll out the second ball to form a large rectangle. Aim for something roughly 25cm wide and 34cm long. Trim the edges. Spread half the filling down the length of the pastry, leaving a 2cm bare border on either side. Roll up as neatly as you can. Repeat with the remaining pastry and filling. Grab your sharpest knife and cut each roll into slices around 5cm thick. Carefully lift each slice of pastry with a fish slice or a broad palette knife and transfer to the pastry-lined tin, arranging them cut sides up like a posy of roses. This is inevitably a messy old business, with bits dropping out here and there, but don't get dispirited. When the filling falls out, patiently tuck it back into its gaping spiral or between the roses. Keep going, nestling them in tight against each other until the tin is full. Bake for 40 minutes, then cover with foil and return to the oven for a final 15 minutes. Let it cool for 15–20 minutes in the tin, run a narrow knife around the edge, then carefully unmould. Eat warm, or at room temperature.

Susumelle

Chocolate and Almond Biscuits

Susumelle belong to a cluster of Italian biscuits that are baked to a relatively hard consistency, like the more familiar northern *biscotti*, partly for long keeping and partly because they taste so good dipped into a little glass of sweet, fortified wine or a liqueur, or a steaming espresso. Or tea, though that's hardly Italian. If you are a biscuit dunker by nature, then these are for you. If you aren't, try them anyway, to enjoy the chocolate, almondy crunch. Traditionally, *susumelle* are Christmas treats, but in the autumn they become known as *pitte di San Martino*, baked for the saint's feast day on 11 November.

They are easy enough to make but one note of caution: do not overbake! A few minutes too long in the oven produces an unfeasibly tooth-cracking rock-hard biscuit.

Makes 30–35

270g plain flour, plus a little extra for rolling out
15g unsweetened cocoa powder
1 teaspoon ground cinnamon
1 teaspoon baking powder
40g blanched almonds, chopped
finely grated zest of 1 orange
100g caster sugar
100g runny honey
2 tablespoons extra virgin olive oil
50ml water

For the glaze
50g dark chocolate, finely chopped
2 tablespoons extra virgin olive oil

Preheat the oven to 180°C/160°C fan/gas 4. Line a couple of baking trays with baking parchment.

Mix the flour with the cocoa, cinnamon and baking powder. Add the chopped almonds and the orange zest. Put the sugar, honey, olive oil and water into a small pan and heat gently, without letting it boil. Stir until the sugar has dissolved. Pour this into the flour. Mix together to form a soft dough.

Roll the dough out to a thickness of 1cm on a lightly floured board. If you happen to have a leaf-shaped/oval biscuit cutter, get it out of the cupboard and use it to stamp out biscuits. If not, cut the dough into 3cm wide strips, then cut on the diagonal to make diamonds. Lay on the lined baking trays. Gather up the scraps of dough, roll into a ball and roll out again to make more. Bake for 10–12 minutes, until slightly domed and firm but not hard. Transfer to a wire rack and leave to cool.

Put the chocolate and olive oil into a bowl and place over a pan of gently simmering water, making sure that the base does not come into contact with the water. Take the pan off the heat and let the chocolate melt, stirring occasionally. One by one, dip the curved surface of each *susumelle* into the chocolate, then return to the wire rack to cool and set.

Stored in an airtight tin, these will keep for several months.

Recipes Course by Course

Antipasti and contorni

An *antipasto* is either a simple starter, or a collection of small dishes that come before the *primo* course of an Italian meal. *Contorni* are vegetable side dishes. These two categories overlap, with more complex *contorni* often featuring in a mixed *antipasto*.

Fish

Alici Marinate *Marinated Anchovies* (page 26)
Impepata di Cozze *Peppery Mussels* (page 69)
Insalata di Baccalà Crudo *Raw Salt Cod Salad* (page 158)
Melanzane Ripiene al Tonno *Stuffed Aubergines with Tuna* (page 76)

Vegetables

Acquasale *Vegetable and Bread Salad* (page 140)
Cardoncelli Trifolati *Fried King Oyster Mushrooms with Parsley, Wine and Garlic* (page 39)
Carpaccio di Carciofi *Raw Artichoke Salad* (page 208)
Cicerchie e Ceci Neri al Pomodoro *Puglian Beans in Red Wine Tomato Sauce* (page 35)
Cime di Rapa e Capperi in Pastella *Cime di Rapa and Caper Fritters* (page 21)
Cime di Rapa 'Nfucate *Braised Cime di Rapa with Chilli and White Wine* (page 19)
Contadina Sisina's Involtini di Melanzane al Latte di Capra *Aubergine Rolls Baked in Goat's Milk* (page 121)
Insalata di Arance, Finocchi e Olive *Orange, Fennel and Black Olive Salad* (page 142)
Insalata di Cardoncelli e Borlotti *King Oyster Mushroom and Borlotti Bean Salad* (page 38)

Meat

Bread

Primi

Pasta- and rice-based dishes and a few hearty soups.

Fish

Casarecce al Sughetto di Pesce *Casarecce Pasta with a Little Tomato and Fish Sauce* (page 28)

Pasta, Cannellini, Cozze (Estate) *Pasta with Cannellini Beans and Mussels, Summer Version* (page 62)

Riso, Fagioli e Cozze (Inverno) *Rice (or Pasta) with Cannellini Beans and Mussels, Winter Version* (page 60)

Spaghetti al Nero di Seppia *Black Spaghetti with Cuttlefish* (page 256)

Spaghetti al Sugo di Seppie e Piselli *Spaghetti with Slow-Cooked Cuttlefish and Peas* (page 257)

Spaghetti alla San Giuannin *Spaghetti with Anchovy, Olives, Capers and Chilli* (page 153)

Spaghetti alla Seppia *Spaghetti with Cuttlefish* (page 255)

Tumact Me Tulez *Tagliatelle with Walnuts, Tomato and Anchovies* (page 236)

Vegetables

Cialledda Calda *Matera's Winter Vegetable Casserole* (page 123)

Ciambotto in Pane *Ciambotto Picnic Loaf* (page 216)

Cocule di Ricotta e Spinaci *Potato, Ricotta and Spinach Dumplings in Tomato Sauce (with or without horseradish)* (page 67)

La Crapiata *Matera's Bean and Grain Soup* (page 145)

Pomodorini Scattariciati *Exploding Tomatoes* (page 33)

Spaghetti all'Assassina *Assassin's Spaghetti* (page 64)

Meat

Ditaloni Rigati con Fave Fresche, Finocchio, Pancetta *Pasta with Broad Beans, Fennel and Pancetta* (page 248)

Fileja alla Silana *Pasta with Sausage and Porcini* (page 231)

Orecchiette e Cavolfiore *Orecchiette with Cauliflower and Pancetta* (page 55)

Pasta China *Baked Pasta with Meatballs, Cheese and Hot Sausage* (page 242)

Pasta alla Mollica con Salsiccia e Peperoni Cruschi *Pasta with Breadcrumbs, Sausage and Paprika* (page 177)

Pasta alla Pastora *Pasta with Ricotta, Pecorino and Pancetta (or Sausage)* (page 240)

Zuppa di Borlotti, Bietole, Patate e 'Nduja *Borlotti, Swiss Chard, Potato and 'Nduja Soup* (page 222)

Secondi

Main courses, usually served with basic vegetable *contorni*, or no accompaniment at all.

Fish

Alici, Orata o Spigola Arracanate *Roast Anchovy, Sea Bream or Sea Bass Fillets with Breadcrumbs, Mint and Capers* (page 24)

Baccalà Fritto con Cipolle e Ceci *Fried Salt Cod with Onions and Chickpeas* (page 163)

Baccalà con Pomodoro e Olive *Salt Cod with Cherry Tomatoes and Green Olives* (page 159)

Baccalà con Pomodoro, Olive e Sultanina *Salt Cod with Tomatoes, Olives and Sultanas* (page 161)

Impepata di Cozze *Peppery Mussels* (page 69)

Melanzane Ripiene al Tonno *Stuffed Aubergines with Tuna* (page 76)

Pesce San Pietro al Forno con Asparagi, Olive e Arance *Roast John Dory (or Sea Bream) with Asparagus, Orange and Olives* (page 167)

Pesce Spada alla Ghiotta *Swordfish with Potatoes, Tomato, Capers and Olives* (page 261)

Tonno in Agrodolce *Seared Tuna with Sweet-Sour Onions, Mint and Pinenuts* (page 263)

Vegetables

Cialledda Calda *Matera's Winter Vegetable Casserole* (page 123)
Cocule di Ricotta e Spinaci *Potato, Ricotta and Spinach Dumplings in Tomato Sauce (with or without horseradish)* (page 67)
Falagoni Lucani *Lucanian Pasties* (page 148)
Mulingiani Chjini *Very Cheesy Stuffed Aubergines, Calabrian Style* (page 75)

Meat

Capretto Al Forno *Roast Kid* (page 238)
Coniglio alla Cacciatora *Rabbit with White Wine and Mushrooms* (page 169)
Manzo alla Maniera della Moglie del Macellaio *Pot Roast Beef with Dried Red Peppers and Pancetta* (page 175)
Matera's Pignata di Pecora *Lamb, Potato and Vegetable Casserole* (page 180)
Melanzane Ripiene di Carne *Stuffed Aubergines Maria-Downstairs Style* (page 72)
Petto di Pollo Ripieno di 'Nduja e Ricotta *Chicken Stuffed with 'Nduja and Wrapped in Prosciutto Crudo* (page 224)
Stracetti di Agnello *Sautéed Lamb with Crisp Breadcrumbs* (page 78)
U Pastizz R'Tunnar *Rotondella's Pork Pasties* (page 151)

Dolci

Puddings and pastries.

Bignè di San Giuseppe *St Joseph's Fritters* (page 94)
Calzoncelli di Castagne *Chestnut and Chocolate Fritters* (page 189)
Calzone di Ricotta *Ricotta, Chocolate and Candied Peel Pie* (page 185)
Cartellate *Honey Drizzled Christmas Spirals* (page 101)

Bread, Conserves and Everything Else

Acknowledgements

A mighty thank you to all who have led me through these lands of sunshine, winds and storms, to friends and strangers who drop pearls of information and encouragement in my lap. Thank you to the generous cooks and hosts who have revealed recipes and locations, stories and routes throughout Puglia, Basilicata and Calabria.

A huge thank you to my editor, Lindsey Evans at Headline, for her phenomenal patience, and to my agent Heather Holden-Brown for gently turning my nose back to the grindstone every now and then.

Thank you to friends in Ceglie Messapica: to Francesca who feeds and strokes my cats when I'm not here, to Veronica who waves from her balcony opposite mine, to Downstairs Maria, to David and Fran and Filomena, to Siobhan and Stephen, to all at Bar del Teatro and Innamorata and, above all, to Rhona and Julien (even though you abandoned us).

Conversion charts

Weight

25/30g	1oz	150g	5½oz	450g	1lb
40g	1½oz	200g	7oz	500g	1lb 2oz
50g	1¾oz	225g	8oz	600g	1lb 5oz
55g	2oz	250g	9oz	750g	1lb 10oz
70g	2½oz	300g	10½oz	900g	2lb
85g	3oz	350g	12oz	1kg	2lb 4oz
100g	3½oz	375g	13oz	2kg	4lb 8oz
115g	4oz	400g	14oz		

Length

5mm	¼ inch	10cm	4 inches
1cm	½ inch	15cm	6 inches
2cm	¾ inch	20cm	8 inches
2.5cm	1 inch	23cm	9 inches
3cm	1¼ inches	25cm	10 inches
5cm	2 inches	28cm	11 inches
8cm	3¼ inches	30cm	12 inches

Volume: liquids

5ml	–	1 tsp
15ml	½ fl oz	1 tbsp
30ml	1 fl oz	2 tbsp
60ml	2 fl oz	¼ cup
75ml	2½ fl oz	⅓ cup
120ml	4 fl oz	½ cup
150ml	5 fl oz	⅔ cup
175ml	6 fl oz	¾ cup
225ml	8 fl oz	1 cup
350ml	12 fl oz	1½ cups
500ml	18 fl oz	2 cups
1 litre	1¾ pints	4 cups

Volume: dry ingredients – an approximate guide

Flour	125g	1 cup
Butter	225g	1 cup (2 sticks)
Breadcrumbs (dried)	125g	1 cup
Nuts	125g	1 cup
Seeds	160g	1 cup
Dried fruit	150g	1 cup
Dried pulses (large)	175g	1 cup
Grains & small pulses	200g	1 cup
Sugar	200g	1 cup

Oven temperatures

°C	with fan	°F	gas mark
110°C	90°C	225°F	¼
120°C	100°C	250°F	½
140°C	120°C	275°F	1
150°C	130°C	300°F	2
160°C	140°C	325°F	3
180°C	160°C	350°F	4
190°C	170°C	375°F	5
200°C	180°C	400°F	6
220°C	200°C	425°F	7
230°C	210°C	450°F	8
240°C	220°C	475°F	9

Index